First World War
and Army of Occupation
War Diary
France, Belgium and Germany

20 DIVISION
Headquarters, Branches and Services
Royal Army Veterinary Corps
Assistant Director Veterinary Services
20 July 1915 - 18 March 1919

WO95/2104/3

The Naval & Military Press Ltd
www.nmarchive.com
Published in association with The National Archives

Published by

The Naval & Military Press Ltd

Unit 10 Ridgewood Industrial Park,

Uckfield, East Sussex,

TN22 5QE England

Tel: +44 (0) 1825 749494

www.naval-military-press.com

www.nmarchive.com

This diary has been reprinted in facsimile from the original. Any imperfections are inevitably reproduced and the quality may fall short of modern type and cartographic standards.

© Crown Copyright
Images reproduced by permission of The National Archives, London, England, 2015.

Contents

Document type	Place/Title	Date From	Date To
Heading	2104/3 Asst Div Vetinary Services		
Heading	20th Division Asst Dir. Vety Service Jly 1915-Mar 1919		
Miscellaneous	AVE 20th Division.		
War Diary	Larkhill	20/07/1915	22/07/1915
War Diary	Lumbres	23/07/1915	27/07/1915
War Diary	Lynde	27/07/1915	28/07/1915
War Diary	Merris	31/07/1915	27/08/1915
War Diary	Nouvear Naud	28/08/1915	21/11/1915
War Diary	Sailly	24/11/1915	03/03/1916
War Diary	Sheet 28 A 22.d.8.3.	11/03/1916	30/06/1916
War Diary	Poperinghe	01/07/1916	15/07/1916
War Diary	Esquelbecq	16/07/1916	20/07/1916
War Diary	Bailleul	21/07/1916	24/07/1916
War Diary	Doulens	25/07/1916	26/07/1916
War Diary	Bus-Les-Artois	27/07/1916	28/07/1916
War Diary	Couin	29/07/1916	31/07/1916
War Diary	Couin	01/08/1916	17/08/1916
War Diary	Beauval	18/08/1916	20/08/1916
War Diary	Treux	21/08/1916	21/08/1916
War Diary	F.26.d.2.2	22/08/1916	23/08/1916
War Diary	Citadel	24/08/1916	31/08/1916
War Diary	Citadel Near Fricourt	01/09/1916	05/09/1916
War Diary	Hrbre Fourche	06/09/1916	06/09/1916
War Diary	Corbie	07/09/1916	11/09/1916
War Diary	Arbre Fourche	12/09/1916	17/09/1916
War Diary	Citadel	18/09/1916	21/09/1916
War Diary	Fnaked Tree Camp	22/09/1916	22/09/1916
War Diary	Treux	23/09/1916	27/09/1916
War Diary	Arbre Fourche	28/09/1916	30/09/1916
Heading	A.D.V.S. 20th Division October 1916 Vol 5		
War Diary	Arbre Fourchel L.2.b. Albert Sheet	01/10/1916	06/10/1916
War Diary	Citadel	07/10/1916	09/10/1916
War Diary	Treux	10/10/1916	15/10/1916
War Diary	Corbie	16/10/1916	19/10/1916
War Diary	Vignacourt	20/10/1916	21/10/1916
War Diary	Belloy	22/10/1916	31/10/1916
War Diary	Belloy	01/11/1916	01/11/1916
War Diary	Cavillon	02/11/1916	15/11/1916
War Diary	Corbie	16/11/1916	24/11/1916
War Diary	Con	25/11/1916	30/11/1916
War Diary	Corbie	01/12/1916	12/12/1916
War Diary	4.2 D.9.7	13/12/1916	31/12/1916
Heading	War Diary Of the A.D.V.S. 20th Division January 1917 Vol 8		
War Diary	Corbie	01/01/1917	04/01/1917
War Diary	Minden Post	05/01/1917	28/01/1917
War Diary	Heilly	29/01/1917	31/01/1917
Heading	War Diary of A.D.V.S. 20th Division February 1917 Vol 9		

War Diary	Heilly	01/02/1917	09/02/1917
War Diary	A.2.d.9.7	10/02/1917	28/02/1917
Heading	War Diary of A.D.V.S. 20th Division March 1917 Vol 10		
War Diary	A.2.d.9.7	01/03/1917	19/03/1917
War Diary	A.4.d.5.2	20/03/1917	31/03/1917
Heading	War Diary A.D.V.S. 20th Division April 1917 Vol XI		
War Diary	A.4.d.5.2 Sheet Albert	01/04/1917	03/04/1917
War Diary	Rocquigny	04/04/1917	30/04/1917
Heading	War Diary May 1917 Vol 12 A.D.V.S. 20th Division.		
War Diary	Ytres (P.26.b.5.0) 57c 1.40.000	01/05/1917	10/05/1917
War Diary	Ytres	11/05/1917	23/05/1917
War Diary	The Monument	24/05/1917	31/05/1917
Heading	War Diary of ADVS 20th Divn June 1917		
War Diary	The Monument H.15.c	01/06/1917	30/06/1917
Heading	War Diary DADVS July 1917 Vol 14		
War Diary	Bernaville	01/07/1917	08/07/1917
War Diary	Domart	09/07/1917	21/07/1917
War Diary	Proven	22/07/1917	31/07/1917
War Diary	Dragon Camp	07/08/1917	19/08/1917
War Diary	Proven	20/08/1917	31/08/1917
War Diary	Proven	01/09/1917	11/09/1917
War Diary	Melch Farm	12/09/1917	30/09/1917
War Diary	Proven	01/10/1917	02/10/1917
War Diary	Haplincourt	03/10/1917	04/10/1917
War Diary	Peronne	05/10/1917	10/10/1917
War Diary	Sorel Le Grand	11/10/1917	31/10/1917
War Diary	Sorel le Grand	01/11/1917	29/11/1917
War Diary	Amglst Lane	30/11/1917	30/11/1917
War Diary	Sorel-Le-Gd	01/12/1917	04/12/1917
War Diary	Baizieux	05/12/1917	06/12/1917
War Diary	Hucqueliers	07/12/1917	12/12/1917
War Diary	Blaringhem	13/12/1917	07/01/1918
War Diary	Westoutre	08/01/1918	22/02/1918
War Diary	Ercheu	23/02/1918	21/03/1918
War Diary	Ham	22/03/1918	22/03/1918
War Diary	Esmery Hallon	23/03/1918	23/03/1918
War Diary	Nesle	24/03/1918	24/03/1918
War Diary	Carrepuits	25/03/1918	25/03/1918
War Diary	Hangest	26/03/1918	26/03/1918
War Diary	Castel	27/03/1918	27/03/1918
War Diary	Moreuil	28/03/1918	28/03/1918
War Diary	Domart	29/03/1918	29/03/1918
War Diary	Boves	30/03/1918	31/03/1918
War Diary	Sains-En-Amienois	01/04/1918	03/04/1918
War Diary	Quevauvillers	04/04/1918	10/04/1918
War Diary	Huppy Gamaches	12/04/1918	18/04/1918
War Diary	Mingoval	19/04/1918	02/05/1918
War Diary	Villers-Au-Bois	03/05/1918	07/05/1918
War Diary	Chateau de La Haie	08/05/1918	30/06/1918
War Diary	Chateau-De-La-Haie	01/07/1918	06/10/1918
War Diary	Villers Chatel	07/10/1918	31/10/1918
War Diary	Cambrai	01/11/1918	03/11/1918
War Diary	Avesnes	04/11/1918	06/11/1918
War Diary	Vendegies	07/11/1918	08/11/1918
War Diary	Wargnies	09/11/1918	09/11/1918

War Diary	Bavay	10/11/1918	10/11/1918
War Diary	Feignies	11/11/1918	23/11/1918
War Diary	Wargnies Le Grand	24/11/1918	26/11/1918
War Diary	Rieux	27/11/1918	28/11/1918
War Diary	Cambrai	29/11/1918	30/11/1918
War Diary	Pas	01/12/1918	18/03/1919

2104/13
Assi. Dr. Vahmarj Sarris

20TH DIVISION

ASST DIR. VETY SERVICES
JLY 1915. - MAR 1919

A.V.C. 20th Division.

Major C.E. STEEL. — ADVS Joined 14-4-15. Evacuated sick 11-3-16

Major T.L. ISHMAN. — Joined 25-4-15 as O.C. 32 MVS. Appointed ADVS Div 11-3-16. Appointed ADVS 17th Corps 14-2-19 with Rank of Temp. Lt. Col.

Capt W. DENINGTON. (TC) — Joined 22-4-15. Transferred to ALDERSHOT 11-3-18.

Capt F.S. CLAY. (TC) — Joined 9-3-15 as V.O. i/c 92nd Bde RFA until Division during whole of the time in France.

Capt J.B. WELHAM (TC) — Joined 6-1-15. Appointed O.C. 32 MVS 11-3-16. Left took command of 13th Corps VETY. EVACUATING STATION 17-5-18.

LIEUT. M. CARSON (TC) — Joined 14-7-15. Relinquished commission on termination of agreement 22-3-16

LIEUT R. GARLAND. (TC) — Joined 6-1-16. Trnsfd to No 3 Vety Hospital 11-6-16

Capt R.D. WILLIAMS (TF) — Joined 16-3-16. Trnsfd to 47th Div 25-9-16

Lieut. J.M. ALEXANDER (TC)	Joined 24-3-16. Relinquished commission 14-12-16
Lieut. R. G. GRAY (TC)	Joined 16-6-16 Relinquished commission 25-9-16
Capt. A.J. SELLERS (TC)	Joined 15-8-16. Trnsfd to No 3 Vety Hospital. 16-8-17
Lieut. G. FRAYNE (TC)	Joined 3-9-16. Left on 17-2-17 as VO t/ 93rd Bde RFA when that Bde was made an Army Bde
Capt. C. SIMONS (TC)	Joined 20-12-16 Evacuated sick. 30-6-18
Capt. J. J. Addison (TC)	Joined 10-3-18. Still with Division
Capt. P.T LINDSAY (SR)	Joined 15-3-18 as O.C. 32 M.V.S. Appointed D.A.D.V.S. 55th Divn 5-12-18
Capt. W. ANDREW (TC)	Joined 5-8-18 Trnsfd to 232 Army Bde RFA. 10-1-19
Capt. G. K. SHAW (Reg)	Joined 9-12-18 as O.C 32 M.V.S
Capt. J.M. McMASTER (T.F)	Joined 9-1-19.

20.7.15-6 / 30-6.16
Vol I

A.D.V.S., 20th Division

WAR DIARY
or
INTELLIGENCE SUMMARY.
(Erase heading not required.)

Army Form C. 2118.

Instructions regarding War Diaries and Intelligence Summaries are contained in F. S. Regs., Part II. and the Staff Manual respectively. Title pages will be prepared in manuscript.

Place	Date 1915	Hour	Summary of Events and Information	Remarks and references to Appendices
Larkhill	20.7	10.25 AM	Entrained for oversea with 48 horses, 3 vehicles & 36 other ranks. Arrived Southampton	
		2.30		
		4.00 PM	Left Southampton per H.T. Manchester Importer	
	21.7	4.30 AM	Arrived Havre & proceeded to No. 5 Camp.	
		9 PM	Started for Gare de Marchandises, arriving 10 PM & entraining the having learning 2 AM 22nd inst	
	22.7	9 PM	Arrived Lumbres, raining very heavily. Proceeded to find billets & horse lines in by midnight.	
Lumbres	23.7		Wrote D.V.S. Abbeville reporting arrival & giving distribution of the Veterinary Officers of the Divn.	
	24.7		Visited lines of 11th D.L.I. and S.S. Cable Coy. gave help & assistance. Received letter from D.D.V.S. G.H.Q. 2 asking me to inform him if horses are left behind by units	
	26.7		Visited 93rd Brigade R.3a at Acquin	
	27.7	11 AM	Visited Divl Cavalry at Setques	
		3 PM	11th Durham Light Infantry at Esguerdes	
			Lumbres where Headquarters are situated is in a fertile valley surrounded by low hills & downs & following the line of a small river. Good camping ground in small woods. Large quantities of oats, wheat & barley grown here.	

Army Form C. 2118.

WAR DIARY
or
INTELLIGENCE SUMMARY.
(Erase heading not required.)

Instructions regarding War Diaries and Intelligence Summaries are contained in F.S. Regs., Part II. and the Staff Manual respectively. Title pages will be prepared in manuscript.

Place	Date	Hour	Summary of Events and Information	Remarks and references to Appendices
Lynde	27.7		Arrived LYNDE at midday after a march of 11½ miles. Passed through a very fertile country. Left 1 horse of Hd Qr Staff with Brown.	
	28.7	1 pm	Arrived MERRIS. a fine day rather hot. The billeting area is rather wide & well used. The work of the Veterinary officers rather difficult	
MERRIS	31.7		Published in Divl orders extracts from G.R.O. & instructions received from D.D.V.S. 2nd Army transport 10 way of dealing with horses to be evacuated for Veterinary & other reasons. Published in Divl Orders the pamphlet on Glanders received from D.D.V.S. 1st Army. Sent all Veterinary officers a copy of instructions re Mange received from D.D.V.S. 2nd Army. Visited 91st Bde R.F.A. at STAZEEL. There is a great deficiency of water at that place. An endeavour is being made to fix up canvas troughs & a hand pump to supply water from a pond. Published in Divl orders that the Brigade proportion of forage is to be sent with horses which go to the Mobile Vety Section for treatment as rations are drawn 2 days in advance & it is not possible to draw rations for animals sent to M.V.S.	
"	1.8		Visited 70th. 193rd Brigades R.F.A. arrived in 2 horses to M.V.S. cooker for about 2 days instruction. V.O. re making out A form A 2002. The D.D.V.S. inspected the Mobile Vety Section.	

1577 Wt. W10791/1773 500,000 1/15 D.D.&L. A.D.S.S./Forms/C. 2118.

WAR DIARY
or
INTELLIGENCE SUMMARY
(Erase heading not required.)

Army Form C. 2118.

Place	Date	Hour	Summary of Events and Information	Remarks and references to Appendices
MERRIS	2.8.		Visited Rail head to view the road by which an evacuating party would have to proceed. The distance is about 10 miles along a main road carrying a great deal of traffic. Really very sick animals could not be sent except in a float.	
	3.8.		90th Bde RFA & Sqn Inf Brigade of this Division proceed to join the VIIIth Div. also No 1 Sect 9 DAC. Visited the ADVS of the VIIIth Division & informed him of this move. Visited the 93rd Bde RFA & 6th Infantry Brigade. No 2 Vet Ann Columns & found the latter in charge of Lt Clay AVC vice Lt Cavan act to veterinary officer for Lt Clay.	
	6.8.		Sent off 20 horses from Mobile Vet Section 117 (newly returned to DDVS, numbered 3 evacuated 16 dum 8 destroyed)[remaining 117, strength January 3,453 Numbers 1,157]	
	7.8.		Abbeville this week saw 2 outpatients. Cases of mange.	6 Mrs Vety Hospital
	8.8.		Visited units temporarily attached 8th Div. recalled on the RDVS of that Div. to make arrangements. Circulated to all V.O. Circular memo No 40 from D.S.S. re cracked heels.	
	12.8.		Received Circular memo from DDVS/Army No OSG 1609/495 of 7/8/15 re cane grenade helmets for horse. Indented for 5.00 horses. Returned a DADOS. Forwarded memo to OC Mobile Vet Section for his information.	

1577 Wt. W10791/1773 500,000 1/15 D.D.&L. A.D.S.S./Forms/C. 2118.

WAR DIARY or INTELLIGENCE SUMMARY

Army Form C. 2118.

Place	Date	Hour	Summary of Events and Information	Remarks and references to Appendices
Merris	13.8.		Issued Circular memo Coll V.O.S. of Divs of their relation with the Mobile Vety Sections this Div. Sec wkly return 6 DD VS. evacuated 107 cast 68 evacuated to 19 Sw'l Destroyed 2. Remaining 135 Strength M 1234. 26 horses of the Divnl Transport evacuated to Veterinary Hospital Abbeville this morning. Suspected case of mange. The following units are temporarily detached. 90th Bde RFA — The 96th Field Co RE 1 Section Divn Am Column all the 8th Divn. The ADVS of that Div warned accordingly. 1 Battery of 92nd (Howitzer) Brigade attached to the 27th Divn 1st ADVS of that Divn warned.	
"	16.8.		S.S. Cavaly Section now hainsferes to 3rd Corps 1st Divn. The 5.9th Inf Brigade moved today into the 8th Divl Area, also the 62nd Field Ambulance. The 96th Field Co R.E. are already there. The ADVS of that Divn has been warned & Form A sent for. These units have been forwarded for those therein. One Battery of the 92nd Howitzer Brigade is in the 27th Divl area. The ADVS of that Divn has been warned. (135 horses) A Section of the 20th Divl Ammn Column has gone into the 5th Divl Area. Also the ADVS has been warned 106 animals	

WAR DIARY
or
INTELLIGENCE SUMMARY.
(Erase heading not required.)

Army Form C. 2118.

Place	Date	Hour	Summary of Events and Information	Remarks and references to Appendices
Meerut	16.8		In a position like this with regard to the Rail head the absolute necessity of an Ambulance became daily more apparent. It is almost impossible to use a stout tonga. Cases that ought to proceed immediately to railhead have to be kept either in the unit lines or the lines of the Mule het section until they were sufficiently to travel to Rail head which is 8 miles from here. The alternative was destruction to taking into consideration the cost of a flood -, an unnecessary waste of Public money.	
"	20.8 22.8		Went into D.D.V.S. admitted 117 and 87 wounded (2) 26 don't destroyed remaining 146 strength (H 3075 strength (H 373 Issued a Circular memo to all Veterinary Officers of this Division calling their attention to the careless diagnosing of certain Cases send to the Mobile Vety Section.	
"	26.8		Also calling Veterinary Officers attention to the bad shoeing throughout the Division chauking that if shoes are not available removing can be done regularly	

WAR DIARY
or
INTELLIGENCE SUMMARY.

Army Form C. 2118.

Place	Date	Hour	Summary of Events and Information	Remarks and references to Appendices
Morris	26.8		Issued a circular memorandum as the necessity of a uniformity in first aid dressing by all Veterinary Officers for the benefit of the evacuation of Farriers re under them	
	27.8		Weekly return to D.D.V.S. arrived 105 evac 102 evacuated 31 remaining 15 strength FM 31·31	
	28.8		Moves to Murran Mord arrived there by 10 A.M., but Mobile Vety section	
Nouveau Mord			is train road between Savely & Saterens	
	30.8		Moves the Mobile Section about 1 mile N.W. so as on the Salaria Mord - Begun Road	
Nouveau Mord	1.9		Sices arrival overseas 92 horses have been evacuated by mobile Vety Section to L of C { weekly return to D.D.V.S. arrived 103 evac 5 remaining 40 } Instructed by D.D.V.S. to evacuate every hung creatable case Strength FM 40·40	
	2.9		This is being done (91) {weekly return to D.D.V.S. arrived 135 evac 77 evacuated 13 ran 6 }13 remaining 158 Strength FM 40·40	
	10.9		Arrangements have been made for an advanced Veterinary Dressing Post in case of an action taking place, at the place	
	16.9		Injured animals will be collected by the trains of the V.C. sent there evacuated to M.V.S. after dark {weekly return to D.D.V.S. arrived 99 evac 40·45 } instructed M.V.S. what to M 1517 do further Vety evac Strength 42	
	20.9		Went over Dul Mobile Vety Section, forced it almost empty Battly of 2,3" Vountly of Yaros Den	
	21.9		Have sent to M.O. 32 Mobile Vety Section a horse pied reserve	

WAR DIARY
or
INTELLIGENCE SUMMARY.
(Erase heading not required.)

Place	Date	Hour	Summary of Events and Information	Remarks and references to Appendices
	24.9		Sent off weekly return to D.D.V.S. Admitted 124. Cured 106. Evacuated 30 died 1 destroyed 1 remaining 134. Strength H 4627 / M 1266	
	1.10		Weekly return to D.D.V.S. admitted 137 cured 103 evacuated 35 died 6 destroyed 2 remaining 123 Strength H 4643 / M 1358	
	8.10		Weekly return to D.D.V.S. admitted 157 cured 86 evacuated 46 destroyed 4 remaining 140 Strength H 4376 / M 1252	

WAR DIARY
or
INTELLIGENCE SUMMARY.
(Erase heading not required.)

Army Form C. 2118.

Place	Date	Hour	Summary of Events and Information	Remarks and references to Appendices
	11.10		by M.M.P. as a deserrent. It has worked wonders the part of the Divn that cannot be worked. This is the third animal in the last batch of remounts that has been forth with evacuated. Early arrived unfit for work. The other two were a ringbone and a spavin case. As an attempt to prevent kicks + upsets, a Divn Ordr has been issued advising the use of shackles. also advising the tying of horses to single pickeling pegs without heel shackles to help the preventable injuries A.D. took thead who gave average from 33% to 50% the weekly admissions from all causes. Went round the lines of the 90th Bde R.F.A and in some cases of debility from that area. Column to the mobile Vety section. R.A. horses generally have gone back in condition lately Inspected lines of 59th Bde Bryants forms everything in good order.	
	12.40		Insp. 91st Bde R.F.A Ambulant horse cases. two batteries very good. "A" Column waythery send 3 horses & M.I.S with sternily trailer 60th Hy Bde & 83rd Field Cy R.E. Both satisfactory	

WAR DIARY
or
INTELLIGENCE SUMMARY.

Army Form C. 2118.

(Erase heading not required.)

Place	Date	Hour	Summary of Events and Information	Remarks and references to Appendices
	12.10		Heatworks making write stockings, breek in under what seems a very good showing but have not seen it after rain yet.	
	13.10		Visited 3rd Corps Headquarters & saw arrival of the Staff went of Sn I. G.D.	
	15.10		Have been told by OC No.5 Vety Hospital Abbeville that Evacuated from Evacuated horses can not be returned as all units at the Front have their collars sent with remounts & his Division from units as their head collars are also part of their harness. All this is causing unnecessary friction between units & the Mobile Vety Section. Weekly return to D.D.V.S. admitted 160 cured 97 Evacuated 57 No.3. Remaining 163 Strength ⎰H 4361⎱ ⎱M 1240⎰	
	22.10		Weekly return to D.D.V.S. admitted 124 cured 101 Evacuated 31 Remaining 155. Strength ⎰H 4363⎱ ⎱M 1252⎰	

Army Form C. 2118.

WAR DIARY
or
INTELLIGENCE SUMMARY.
(Erase heading not required.)

Instructions regarding War Diaries and Intelligence Summaries are contained in F. S. Regs., Part II. and the Staff Manual respectively. Title pages will be prepared in manuscript.

Place	Date	Hour	Summary of Events and Information	Remarks and references to Appendices
	28.10		Questioned with ref to chaffing by truck. Have arranged that until orders were received. Lorries chauffeurs at best have high built wait until negro were viewed.	
	29/10		Sent off weekly return to D.D.V.S admitted 82 cases 89 wounded 13 died 3 cases 6 remaining 126 Strength { 5th 4355 / M 1249	
	30.10		Went round Sut Train 60/6 & Field Ambulance & Div Am Column with Lt Colonel A/C very few sick, but had cases sent down through to Mobile Vety Sec	
	2.11		Attended conference at Locon with D.D.V.S. many subjects discussed. Agreed that it would be a good thing to inject pol cases with anti tetanic serum. Had a case of Surgical prophte mange from 1903 Sect Sw.QC of the Divr. Thoroughly examined detachings with up 6 now regular reach	
	5.11		Inspected 93rd Bde R.F.A & 61st Inf Bde Animal on the whole looking well but Indians decidedly very muck. Standers all looked well particularly the cob	

WAR DIARY
or
INTELLIGENCE SUMMARY.
(Erase heading not required.)

Army Form C. 2118.

Place	Date	Hour	Summary of Events and Information	Remarks and references to Appendices
	5.11		Sent off weekly return to D.D.V.S. admitted 137 cured 89 wounded 30, died 5; totalling 2 remaining 139 strength {H} 4361 {M} 1250	
	6.11		Inspected 90th Bde R.F.A. & 89th Inf Bde. The Infantry looking in the whole very well. The artillery suffered a good deal in the different batteries.	
	9.11		Proceeded on 7 days leave to England Capt T. Lushman performing my duties for me.	
	16.11		Returned from leave.	
	19.11		Sent off weekly return to D.D.V.S. admitted 171 cured 66 evacuated 64 died 4 remaining 180. Strength {H} 4837 {M} 992. Inspected horse[?] prepared for casting of 91st Bde R.F.A.	
	20.11		Inspected lines & Dept train & S.C. with a view to sending down convalescent army thin horses that have may be for a rest. Sent to M.V.S. 21 debilitated Harse cases.	
	21.11		Inspected C/92 with the same cases. Sent away 14.	

WAR DIARY
or
INTELLIGENCE SUMMARY.
(Erase heading not required.)

Army Form C. 2118.

Place	Date	Hour	Summary of Events and Information	Remarks and references to Appendices
Sailly	24/11/15		Moved into this area today	
	25/11/15		Inspected horses of 23rd Infy. Field Ambce & R.B. & found all the animals in good condition	
	26/11		Sent off weekly return to D.D.V.S. admitted 207. cured 19. #444 & 68 evacuated 130. remaining 182. died & destroyed 2. Strength NCO 980.	
	27/11		Inspected 2nd Am Col. & evacuated 19 animals for a rest.	
	28/11		Visited 3rd Corps M.S. Hospital. J. & S.S. section (Cav) R.S. results attention to inefficient shoeing.	
	29/11		Inspected Div Cavalry horses in good condition. evacuated two lame horses	
	30/11		Inspected G1 Bde R.F.A. found horses on the whole in good condition also 60th By Bde. all their animals in good condition	
	4/12		Sent off A.F.A. 2100 for week ending 2/12/15 admitted 145. Cured 100. evacuated 52. died 1 destroyed 2. remaining 172. Strength NCO 4433 M 938 Visited M.V.S. & impressed on OC the necessity of accurate december of all animals being forwarded to DVC. Sent out circular memo to all FO's y Divisional boundary out the necessity of carefully naming divisions in weekly returns	

WAR DIARY or INTELLIGENCE SUMMARY

Army Form C. 2118.

Place	Date	Hour	Summary of Events and Information	Remarks and references to Appendices
	7.12		Inspected Transport of 59th Inf Brigade. Animals in good condition & apparently well cared for. Horse lines of 10. R.B. not so clean as might be. 11th & R.B. not sufficient progress is being observed in mainly recruits to cut down in the Regt. establishment of 1500 now about in 25 mgs.	
	9.12		Inspected 92nd & 86th Bde R.F.A. Animals & lines well cared for. Also 63rd & 84th Field Coy R.E. Same remarks.	
	10.12		Sent off weekly return to D.D.V.S. Admissions 107 cures 79. Evacuated 42. Few 2 destroyed 1. Remaining 155. Strength S.M. 4494. S.M. 978.	
	14.12 10.30am		Inspected D.A.C. They have recently received along with Do from 46th Div. in an exchange. They were in much worse condition at Col.	
	2.30 pm		Visited 3rd Corps M.T. Dns. also another of 17th Reserve Park mentioned that they have no V.O. with this is a V.O. reunion for 6th Reserve Park at Conference want a my clear.	
	16.12		Inspected Transport of 6th Inf Bde. Animals in good condition well cared for. No S.O. in 12th Lancashire Regt. Great shortage of handy forwards curry combs.	

WAR DIARY or INTELLIGENCE SUMMARY.

Army Form C. 2118.

(Erase heading not required.)

Place	Date	Hour	Summary of Events and Information	Remarks and references to Appendices
	17.12		Sent off weekly return of sick & lame 67 STJ arrested 95. Cured 68 Evacuated 39 Died 8 destroyed 10 strength H 4639. The Large mortality was due to the collapse of a temporary stable M 808. outright & 8 had to be destroyed, 4 were killed	
	21.12		Inspected horses of 93rd Bde. RFA arrived in good condition on the whole. 200 draw mules arrived the x0yc 91c 192c Horses started wintering	
	24.12		Sent off weekly return to D.D.V.S. ad mission 142. cured 76 evacuated 27. Died 2 destroyed 1. Strength H 4768 M 907	
	25.12		Inspected transport animals of 59th Infantry Brigade reported to D.A.D.M.G. that ael. no. 2 in good condition one of those sent to D.Q.C & the others are they are keeping	
	31.12		4000 draw mules arrived also two spare barrels for syringes all V.O. now working at the mortaleriry Weekly return send in admissions 141 cured 66 evacuated 5 Died 3. destroyed 1. Strength 16H 4712 M 902	
	2.1.16		Pointed out to 110 Brig large number of admissions for crocks week, gave hints to keep minimum. Copy of letter sent to all V.Officers	

Army Form C. 2118.

WAR DIARY
or
INTELLIGENCE SUMMARY.
(Erase heading not required.)

ADVS 20th Division

Instructions regarding War Diaries and Intelligence Summaries are contained in F. S. Regs., Part II. and the Staff Manual respectively. Title pages will be prepared in manuscript.

Place	Date	Hour	Summary of Events and Information	Remarks and references to Appendices
	8.1.16		Sent off weekly return for week ending 6.1.16. Admitted 127. Cured 82. Evacuated 59. Died 2. Strength H.f 4605 M. 683 Sick 96	
	12.1.16		Divn evacuating Sailly. H'd Qrs moved & arrived on 12' at Blaringhem	
	14.1.16		Inspected Reserve Park Tractors attached 3rd Corps H'd Qrs	
	21.1.16		Sent off weekly return to D.D.V.S. 1st Army. Admitted 148. Cured 70. Evacuated 26. Died 3. Destroyed 1. Strength H 4674 M 911	
	22.1.16		Left Blaringhem for Orlaers where we arrived same day, leaving 2 horses at Wites & 2 at Blaringhem unfit to move	
	27.2.16		Sent off weekly return to D.D.V.S. 1st Army & weekly to D.D.V.S. 2nd Army. Admitted 162. Cured 113. Evacuated 63. Died 1. Destroyed 2. Strength H 4470 M 806	
	5.2.16		Divn moves to new area. beginning on 2nd reinforcing move by 5th with H'd Qrs at Esquelbecq	
	11.2.16		Sent off weekly return to D.D.V.S. admitted 107. Cured 86. Evacuated 41. Died 3. Destroyed 1. Strength H/4 4437 M 811 6	

WAR DIARY or INTELLIGENCE SUMMARY.

Army Form C. 2118.

(Erase heading not required.)

Place	Date	Hour	Summary of Events and Information	Remarks and references to Appendices
	11.2		Division ordered to take up its position in the line	
	12.2		Head Quarters move to A 22 d 8.3 Sheet 28	
	14.2		Mobile Vety Section (32) moves to K 5 d 8.7 Sheet 27	
	15.2		Move Completed.	
	18.2		Weekly return for week ending 17.2. sent to D.D.V.S. admitted 76. Cured 71. Evacuated 20 Died 5 destroyed 2 Strength M{ $\frac{H}{S}$ } $\frac{4605}{836}$	
	25.2		Weekly return for 24th Sent to D.D.V.S. army Admissions 87 cured 63. Evacuated 24 died 1 destroyed 2. Strength M{ H S } $\frac{4649}{835}$	
	26.2		Inspected 60th Inf Bde transport lines. They were all in fair condition. The approaches to the 12th K.R.R are in a mad dreadful condition. Two Bde's transport are well looked after in every respect. The 11th D.L.I are in good lines & the animals are well looked after & so are the standings. The S.Q. Bell the approaches to their lines are bad. The lines themselves are arrived with the exception of those of the 10th K.R.R + 11 R.B are well cared for. There was too much rains shown a lack of supervision	

WAR DIARY
or
INTELLIGENCE SUMMARY

Place	Date	Hour	Summary of Events and Information	Remarks and references to Appendices
	26.2		Inspected the lines of the 90' Bde RFA: the horses are in good condition & a good deal of labor is being spent on putting the lines in form & c. & an which seem to have been neglected by the preceeding Div. The approaches to all the lines are beyond reproach for mud. It appears that the Div. entering new lines ought to have not seen of this difficulty & provided for their own but their lines as far from the roads as possible.	
	1.3		Inspected part of the 91st Bde RFA i.e. 2 Batteries & the column & both the lines and the horses showed that a reasonable amount of care is taken of them.	
	2.3		Inspected 83rd, 84th, 96th Field Co. R.E. all annual well cared for & the lines also. Inspected the 61st Field Ambulance and they also are well cared for. The units of the 61st Inf Brigade on the whole looked well, but consider that more attention should be paid to watering and feeding. In some units a skin was attempted by carrying it in a few canvas buckets. Iam sure that in this way the animals do not get enough to drink. At the anx carried that I saw there was a want of uniformity in putting some unified from nose bags to the feed, others were not all, some at the same time	

Army Form C. 2118.

WAR DIARY
or
INTELLIGENCE SUMMARY.
(Erase heading not required.)

Instructions regarding War Diaries and Intelligence Summaries are contained in F. S. Regs., Part II. and the Staff Manual respectively. Title pages will be prepared in manuscript.

Place	Date	Hour	Summary of Events and Information	Remarks and references to Appendices
	3.3.16		Men was particularly the case in the 6" Somerset Light Infantry with the result that the animals are losing condition.	
Abt. 25 A.22, I.8,3	11/1/16	—	Sent off weekly return to D.D.V.S. advanced $\frac{415}{2}$ evac 79 evacuated 11 died & destroyed 1. Strength 4747– $\begin{cases} M\} & 8.35 \\ P\} 2 \end{cases}$ evacuated sick and Major Steel, A.D.V.S., 20th Division, A.V.C. took over duties of A.D.V.S. Capt. T. Lishman, A.V.C.	
"	12/1/16	—	Capt. E. J. B. Welham, A.V.C. relinquished veterinary charge of the 90th & 91st Bdes R.F.A. & assumed command of No 32 Mobile Veterinary Section.	
"	14/1/16	—	Inspected the lines of 60th Infty Bde. Transport, the 59th, 60th & 61st Machine gun Companies. The lines of the 59th M.G.C. & the animals very good, the other two not so good. Inspected the animals & lines of the 11th D.L.I.	
"	15/1/16	—	Inspected 59th Infty Bde. & visited Mob. Vety. Sect.	
"	16 "	—	Inspected horses of Div. Hqrs, R.A. Hdqrs., Div. Signals, & No 1 Sect. D.A.C.	
"	17 "	—	Making out returns.	

WAR DIARY
or
INTELLIGENCE SUMMARY.
(Erase heading not required.)

Army Form C. 2118.

Place	Date	Hour	Summary of Events and Information	Remarks and references to Appendices
Sheet 28 A.22.d.8.3	18/3/16	—	Inspected with the V.O. & R.E., 1st Dgst., 83rd Field Coy. R.E., 84th Fd. Coy R.E., 96th Fd. Coy. R.E., & 61st Infty. Bde & 61st Fd Ambulance.	
"	19/3/16	—	Visited 59th, 60th, & 61st Machine Gun Coys & Mob. Vety. Section.	
"	20/3/16	—	Visited No 2 & 3 Section D.A.C., & Div. Mounted Troops.	
"	21/3/16	—	Visited 158, 159, 160, & 161 Coys A.S.C., & Mob. Vety. Sect.	
"	22/3/16	—	Visited Machine Gun Coys, 20th Div. Sigs., R.A. Hqrs., 20th Div. Hqrs., & M.M.P. Rooms.	
"	23/3/16	—	Visited the D.A.C. with C.R.A. & D.D.R. Second Army.	
"	24/3/16	—	Visited 60th Infty. Bde. Making out returns.	
"	25/3/16	—	Finished returns & visited Div. Mounted Troops.	
"	26/3/16	—	Visited 1 & 2 Section Div. Ammn. Col.	
"	27/3/16	—	Maltreating mules of M.G. Coys.	
"	29"	—	All Hqrs of Div., M.G. Coys, & 60th Infty Bde.	

WAR DIARY
or
INTELLIGENCE SUMMARY.
(Erase heading not required.)

Army Form C. 2118.

Place	Date	Hour	Summary of Events and Information	Remarks and references to Appendices
—	2/4/16		Visited Div R.A, R.E, Headquarters horses, Machine gun Companies and Mob. Vety. sect.	
—	3"		Visited 20th K.R.R., Nos 2 & 3 sect. D.A.C., & 11th D.L.I.	
—	4"		61st Fld Ambulance, 96th Field Coy R.E., 92nd Bde R.F.A, Amm Col & 61st Machine Gun Coy.	
—	5"		Visited 60th Infty Bde.	
—	7"		Busy with returns	
—	8"		Visited 'B' Batty 91st Bde R.F.A.	
—	9"		Visited Machine Gun Companies & Mob. Vety. sect. Visited all Headquarters & 61st Fld. Ambulance.	
—	11"		11th D.L.I. & 20th K.R.R.C.	
—	11"		Capt W. Dennington A.V.C. went into Hospital.	
—	12"		B 91st Brigade R.F.A. & 91st Bde. H.Qrs, Capt R.D. Williams A.V.C. went on 5 days special leave.	
—	13"			
—	14"		Visited 61st Infty Bde & Mob. Vety sect.	

WAR DIARY
or
INTELLIGENCE SUMMARY.
(Erase heading not required.)

Army Form C. 2118.

Place	Date	Hour	Summary of Events and Information	Remarks and references to Appendices
—	15"	"	Visited 5 & 9th Infty. Bde.	
—	18"	"	Moved with the Division to Esquelbecq.	
—	19"	"	In absence of Capt. Pennington took over 5-9th Infty. Bde. M.G.C., 159 Coy. A.S.C., 60th Field Ambulance, 96th Field Coy. R.E. & 62nd Field Ambulance	
—	23"	"	Visited 91st Bde. R.F.A. & Mob. Vety. Sect.	
—	24"	"	Visited 90th Bde. "	
—	26	"	Mob. Vety. Sect.	
—	27	"	Visited 93rd Bde. R.F.A.	
—	28	"	Visited 92nd Bde. R.F.A.	

WAR DIARY
or
INTELLIGENCE SUMMARY.

Army Form C. 2118.

Place	Date	Hour	Summary of Events and Information	Remarks and references to Appendices
—	1/7/16	—	Visited 9/1st & 93rd Bde R.F.A. with D.D.V.S. Second Army. Beginning with Reserve.	
—	4"	—	Visited 20th K.R.R., 20th Signals, A/Batty 93rd Bde R.F.A.	
—	6"	—	Visited 59th Infy Bde.	
—	7"	—	11th D.L.I., 20th K.R.R. & 60th Field Ambulance.	
—	8"	—	Capt. Wellam, A.V.C. went on 7 days leave.	
—	10"	—	60th Infty Bde A.M.V.S.	
—	11"	—	Mob. Vety. Sect.	
—	15"	—	Visited All Divn Headquarters & 158 Bgy A.I.C.	
—	18"	—	Capt. Wellam returned.	
—	20"	—	Divisional Headquarters moved to Poperinghe.	
—	21"	—	Took over 14th Corp H.Q., Signal, M.M.P. & Cavalry. Also 14th Corp, Heavy Brigade Artillery, 177th Tunnelling Coy., 213 Army Troops Coy R.E., 12th Labour Batt., 1st Siege Coy. R.E.	
—	26	—	Visited 61st Infty Bde.	

Place	Date	Hour	Summary of Events and Information	Remarks and references to Appendices
—	27"	—	83rd, 84th & 96th Field Coys. R.E.	
—	30"	—	Visited Corps Headquarters & Corps Cavalry.	

Army Form C. 2118.

WAR DIARY
or
INTELLIGENCE SUMMARY.
(Erase heading not required.)

Instructions regarding War Diaries and Intelligence Summaries are contained in F. S. Regs., Part II. and the Staff Manual respectively. Title pages will be prepared in manuscript.

Place	Date	Hour	Summary of Events and Information	Remarks and references to Appendices
—	1/6	—	Visited 39th Infty Bde. Lt Galand left on 7 days leave	
—	3 "	—	Visited Houthurghe area & saw 6 Battery R.F.A.	
—	5 "	—	Visited Corp. sect. & Corp. Headquarters. Lt Gray A.V.C. arrived. Mobile Vety. sect & Police Horse at Vlamertinghe	
—	7 "	—	Corps Cavalry	
—	8 "	—	Lt Galand returning. Visited 60 Infty Bde	
—	10 "	—	Lt Galand departed for No 5 Vety. Hospital, Boulogne	
—	11 "	—	Visited Corp Cavalry	
—	12 "	—	Visited Mob. Vety. Sect & Corp Cavalry	
—	14 "	—	Visited No 3 section of 20th Div. Amm. Col?	
—	15 "	—	Visited Mobile Vety. section, XV th Corp Headquarters and	
—	16 "	—	Cavalry	
—	17 "	—	Visited 59 th Infantry Bde. Transport Lines	
—	18 "	—	Obtained 7 days leave to England and instructed Capt Denington A.V.C. to act for me.	
—	19 "	—	Went on leave	
—	26 "	—	Returned from leave	

Army Form C. 2118.

WAR DIARY
or
INTELLIGENCE SUMMARY.
(Erase heading not required.)

Place	Date	Hour	Summary of Events and Information	Remarks and references to Appendices
	27/6		Visited Mobile Vety. Sect. Corps Cavalry & XIVth Corps Headquarters.	
	28/6		Visited Headquarters of Div, R.A., R.E., M.M.P. & Signal.	
			Attended conference of DDVS, 2nd Army at Bailleul.	
	29/6		Visited No 3 sick horse halt. Visited Bandhook, an opening to see civilian horse injured by a government lorry. Capt. Hamilton A.V.C. (T.C.) arrived to take over charge of XIVth Corps H.Qrs & Cavalry.	
	30/6		Whole of morning taken up with showing Capt. Hamilton his new charge. The remainder of the day occupied with the weekly return of sick & injured.	

T. Litchman
Major A.V.C.,
A.D.V.S., 20th Div.

War Diary of A.D.V.S. 20 Division
July
Vol 2

WAR DIARY
or
INTELLIGENCE SUMMARY.
(Erase heading not required.)

Army Form C. 2118.

Place	Date	Hour	Summary of Events and Information	Remarks and references to Appendices
POPERINGHE	1/7/16		Inspected the animals and standing of the 59th & 60th Infantry Brigades and their respective Machine Gun Companies. Everything found to be satisfactory excepting the standing of the 10th Batt. Rifle Bde. A.F.A.2000 sent to D.D.V.S. A.F.B.158 sent to Officer i/c A.V.C. Base Records G.H.Q. 3rd Echelon. Forwarded indent for Veterinary Stores.	
"	2 "		Sent Circular Memo. to all V.O.s in Division complaining of the inability of many Regtl. A.V.C. to give a chloral hydrate ball in a proper manner, with the result that many animals afterwards show irritation of the mouth. Also calling attention to the fact that when it is necessary to give a chloral hydrate ball in solution not less than a quart of water should be used for 1 Ball. Inspected the standings and animals of 11th Batt. D.L.I. and found everything satisfactory. Visited the Mobile Veterinary Section.	
"	3 "		Inspected animals of Nos. 2 & 4 sections of the 25th Div. Ammn. Col. & found all satisfactory. Visited W.252 M.V. Vet. Section. Despatched 1 sergt. walleyed to A.D.V.S. 1st Australian Division.	
"	4 "		Inspected the horses and standings of the 13th Group H.A. Ammn. Col. North Midland H.A., 141st Batt. H.A., 132 Batty. H.A. & 20th Signal Coy R.A.	
"	5 "		Inspected horses and standings of B Batty. 91st Bde. R.F.A. & No.32 Mobile Veterinary Section. Visited No.2 Section of the 20th Div. Ammn Col. in compliance with instructions from D.D.V.S. second Army to check an Officers Chest left by 14th Div. Ammn. Col. & found by the 28th D.A.C.	

WAR DIARY
or
INTELLIGENCE SUMMARY.
(Erase heading not required.)

Army Form C. 2118.

Place	Date	Hour	Summary of Events and Information	Remarks and references to Appendices
Poperinghe	5/7/16		(continued) Sent out to all V.O.s in the Division a circular asking them to report such cases as debility &c. that are not urgent, so that they will reach the M.V.S. before Sunday(?), as if they are sent in on Sundays the weekly batch are left by road for Receiving Hospital at all hours, they have to be kept at the M.V.S. for a week & cause congestion. Also a circular giving instructions as to Vety. administration during moving warfare.	
"	6/7/16		Inspected the animals and standings of Nos 1 & 3 Sections of the Div. Amm. Col.; also 'B' Batty. 90th Bde R.F.A., & 'B' Batty. 93rd Brigade R.F.A. Visited Mobile Veterinary Section.	
"	7/7/16		Inspected horses and standings of 'A' Batty. 91st Bde R.F.A., 61st Field Ambulance, & 12th Labour Battalion. Visited No 32 Mobile Veterinary Section. Checking A.F.A 2000 from the Vety. Officers.	
"	8/7/16		Busy with the weekly return (A.F.A 2000) for the Division. 71 cases admitted during the week, 49 were cured, 8 transferred sick, 3 died, & 2 destroyed. Attended the weekly conference with the A.D.Ss Division at 2-30 p.m.	
"	9/7/16		Inspected the animals & standings of 158, 159, 160 & 161 Coys. A.S.C. & found all satisfactory.	

WAR DIARY
or
INTELLIGENCE SUMMARY.

(Erase heading not required.)

Army Form C. 2118.

Place	Date	Hour	Summary of Events and Information	Remarks and references to Appendices
POPERINGE.	10/7/16		Inspected the horses & standings of 'B' Batty. 92nd Bde. R.F.A. Found a shortage of head chains & many animals tied to their lines by means of hay wire. The head ropes that are used should be stopped in some sort of unpleasant material to prevent animals eating them. If a new rope is put on a horse it eats through it in a very few minutes. The animals are not fed in the morning until 8 am. after doing two hour exercise. It was advised that at least half a feed should be given before they are taken out. Also inspected the animals and standings of 'C' Batty. 90th Bde. R.F.A. and 'A' Batty. 93rd Bde. R.F.A. & found them in good condition. The horse feet in 'A' 93 were found rather long & instruction was given to remedy this. Visited Mobile Vety. Section.
"	11/7/16		Rode to HOUTKERQUE and inspected the horses & lines of the following units: Hd. Qrs. of the 92nd & 93rd Bde. R.F.A. 'D' Batty 90th Bde. R.F.A.; 'D' 91st R.F.A.; 'C' 92 R.F.A., 'C' & 'D' 93rd R.F.A. Found all satisfactory.
"	12/7/16		Visited Divisional Headquarter Horses, R.A. H.Q. Horses, R.E. H.Q. Horses & Div M.M.P.
"	13/7/16		Nothing to record.

WAR DIARY
or
INTELLIGENCE SUMMARY.
(Erase heading not required.)

Army Form C. 2118.

Place	Date	Hour	Summary of Events and Information	Remarks and references to Appendices
POPERINGE	14/7/16	—	Got in all returns & checked them. The day was interrupted by the enemy gunfire on the Town necessitating the shifting of Div. H.Q. into a camp outside of the town.	
"	15/7/16	—	Making out the consolidated A.F.A. 2000 and arranging for the Divisional move into Corps Reserve.	
ESQUELBECQ	16/7/16	—	The whole day occupied with the move from POPERINGE to ESQUELBECQ.	
"	17/7/16	—	The Mobile Veterinary Section moved from " to ". Visited the 5th Labour Batt. at REXPOEDE and arrived at 7 p from munition Hoomeghinurus and saw a case of munition Haemoglobinuria. Visited Mobile Vety. Sect. at 6.27.a.7.7, sheet 27, 1:40,000 and the 5th Labour Batt.	
"	18/7/16	—	Visited the horse and stables of 20th Div. HQRqrs., R.E. HdQrs, M.M.P, 20th Div. Sig. Coy. & No 32 Mob. Vety. Sect.	
"	19/7/16	—	The 20th Div. less 20th Div. Artillery & 60th Infty. Bde., marched from ESQUELBECQ to BAILLEUL. Owing to 24th Div. M.V.S. not having moved No 32 M.V.S. was billeted for the night near St Jan Capel.	
"	20/7/16	—	The Mobile Vety. Sect. moved into sheet 36, B.I.d.8.6. after the 24th Div. M.V.S. had moved out. Visited M.V.S. with D.D.V.S., Second Army. Visited 60th Fd. Ambulance, 159 & 161 Coys A.S.C. 36th Div Artillery arrived.	
BAILLEUL	21/7/16	—		
"	22/7/16	—	Made out return for the week. Explained the area to the A.D.V.S. of the 36th Div.	

WAR DIARY
or
INTELLIGENCE SUMMARY.
(Erase heading not required.)

Army Form C. 2118.

Place	Date	Hour	Summary of Events and Information	Remarks and references to Appendices
BAILEUL	23/7/16		Division preparing to move. Mobile Vety. Section moved out to Stynbecke Cappel on the Caoel Road. Handed over office and M.V.S. billet to A.D.V.S., 36th Division.	
"	24/7/16		Arranging movement. Left Bailleul for DOULLENS.	
DOULLENS	25/7/16		Took a billet at GROUCHES, about 3 miles W.E. of DOULLENS. The M.V.S. arrived by train at 11-45 p.m. and the Mob. Vety. Sect. marched to its billet.	
"	26/7/16		The Division moved from DOULLENS to BUS-lès-ARTOIS. The Mob. Vety. Sect. moved from GROUCHES to A Camp COUIN. Inspected the animals of Div. Headquarters. Visited the A.D.V.S. of the 38th Division & No 49 Mob. Vety. Sect. to arrange the relief.	
BUS-lès-ARTOIS	27/7/16		D.D.V.S. of Reserve Army called to explain the working of the area. Received the A.F., A.2008 for the week. Found a billet at 1, ST LEGER—	
"	28/7/16		LES-AUTHIE for the Mob. Vety. Sect.	
COUIN	29/7/16		The Div. H.Q. moved to COUIN. The Mob. Vety. Sect. moved to ST LEGER-LES-AUTHIE. Sent in weekly returns to D.D.V.S. Reserve Army.	
"	30/7/16		Visited THIEVRES to examine a dog that had bitten a Private in R.W.F. Arranged the various Vety. charges of the Division in the new area.	
"	31/7/16		Visited the Mob. Vety. Section & also the Veterinary offices &c. Advanced lines of XIVth. Corps Heavy artillery and arranged with the latter the Veterinary service in connection.	

T. Lishman, Major A.V.C.
A.D.V.S. 20 Division

WAR DIARY or INTELLIGENCE SUMMARY.

Army Form C. 2118.

War Diary of A.D.V.S, 20th Div. for August 1916

Vol 3

Place	Date	Hour	Summary of Events and Information	Remarks and references to Appendices
COUIN	1/8/16	—	Inspected the horses and standing of the S.A.A. Section of the 20th D.A.C., 48th Heavy Artillery, & "B" Batty, 121st Bde. R.F.A.	
"	2/8/16	—	Inspected horses and standing of 62nd Field Ambulance, Div. Head-quarters, 20th Signal Coy, & one change with 57th Infty. Bde. from 19th D.R. Reserve Army. Arranged for Mobile Veterinary Section to collect a float car near DOULLENS.	
"	3/8/16	—	Inspecting the standing & horses of 119th & 121st Brigades of the 38th Division R.A. All are in fairly good condition except "B" Batty, 121st Bde. R.F.A.	
"	4/8/16	—	Inspected the horses and standing of 120th & 122nd Bdes, 38th Division Royal Artillery. Conferred with V.O. & received the A.F. A 2000	
"	5/8/16	—	Visited 60th Infantry Bde. & 159 Coy A.S.E. with D.D.R., Reserve Army. Made out & sent in the completed A.F.A 2000 for the Div. Weekly conference with the Q.V.C. 20th Div.	
"	6/8/16	—	Annual circular pointing out necessity for early evacuation of all cases of mange.	
"	7/8/16	—	Artillery of 38th Div. being relieved by Guards Div. Artillery.	
"	8/8/16	—	Relief by Guards Div. R.A. completed. Inspected standing & horses of all Headquarter units.	

WAR DIARY
INTELLIGENCE SUMMARY.
(Erase heading not required.)

Army Form C. 2118.

Place	Date	Hour	Summary of Events and Information	Remarks and references to Appendices
COUIN	9/7/16	—	Inspected standings to animals of 6th & 7th Infantry Bde., 11th D.L.i., 83rd, 84th & 96th Field Coys. R.E., 159, 160 & 161 Coys A.S.C., 60th Machine Gun Coy., & N°2 Sect. Of 4 6th Reserve Park.	
"	10/7/16		Inspected the animals and standings of the 59th Infantry Bde., 62nd Field Ambulance, and 158th Coy A.S.C. The Infantry Transport animals & the mules of the Machine Gun Coy. had very long feet and the shoeing of which were ordered to take place at the earliest time of shoeing.	
"	11/7/16		Inspected the animals & standings of the 60th Infantry Bde. & the small Arm section of the 20th D.A.C. Making out A.F.A.2090	
"	12/7/16		Inspected Vety. Wallets of the Art. & Field Coys. R.E. Sent in to D.D.V.S., Reserve Army the consolidated A.F.A. 2000. Attended a conference with the G.O.C., 20th Division.	
"	13/7/15		Nothing to record	
"	14/7/15		Inspected animals & standings of Div. Headquarters, R.E. H.d Qrtrs, 20th Signal Coy, A.M.M.P.	
"	15/7/15		Lt. R.G. GRAY, A.V.C. (T.C.) left for England on termination of agreement and Capt. A.J. SELLER, A.V.C. (T.C.) reported his arrival, joined in the mounts for Vety. requisites for the Division.	
"	16/7/16		Arranged for Mobile Vety. Section mining a Guard on Div. M.V.S. Establishment. Collect. Attending to sundry office work.	

WAR DIARY
or
INTELLIGENCE SUMMARY.

(Erase heading not required.)

Army Form C. 2118.

Place	Date	Hour	Summary of Events and Information	Remarks and references to Appendices
COUIN	17/8/16	—	Left with the 20th Division to march to Beauval.	
BEAUVAL	18/8/16	—	arrived at Beauval.	
"	20/8/16	—	Marched from Beauval to TREUX.	
TREUX	21/8/16	—	Moved from Treue to F.26.d.2.2. Albert (combined) shut the Mob. Veterinary section moved to Treue.	
F.26.d.2.2.	22/8/16	—	9.D.V.S, Fourth Army called. M.V.S. moved to Meaulte.	
"	23/8/16	—	Div. Headquarters moved to the Citadel.	
Citadel	24/8/16	—	Visiting new transport lines and establishing the office. Had a visit of No 32 Mob. Vety. Sect. published in orders.	
"	25/8/16	—	Received the A.E. A.2060 from the Vety. Officer, & inspected the animals of the S.A.A. section of the 20th Div Amm. Col.	
"	26/8/16	—	Making out returns to inspecting animals and standings of Div Hd.Qrtr, R.E. Hd.Qrtr, M.M.P.	
"	27/8/16	—	Nothing to record.	
"	28/8/16	—	Visited Mob. Vety. Sect. and all Headquarter units & standings.	
"	29/8/16	—	Raining nearly all day. Had most of the horse lines shifted.	
"	30/8/16	—	Very bad weather this morning inspection impossible. Capt. M. Pilkey arrived from HAVRE for duty with 61st Div. Artillery attached to 20th Div.	
"	31/8/16	—	Visited Mobile Veterinary Section & the 24th Bde R.F.A. in connection with an A.V.C. Sergt Wounded to meet by the O.C., Brigade R.F.A. T. Lishman, Maj. A.V.C., A.D.V.S., 20th Div.	

WAR DIARY
or
INTELLIGENCE SUMMARY.

(Erase heading not required.)

Army Form C. 2118.

for September 1916

Place	Date	Hour	Summary of Events and Information	Remarks and references to Appendices
CITADEL near FRICOURT	1/9/16	—	Inspected horses and standings of the 110th, 111th, 112th & 43rd Battery R.F.A., of 6th Div. R.A.	
"	2/9/16	—	Inspected horses and standings of the 21st, 42nd, 53rd & 87th Battery R.F.A. of the 6th Div. R.A.	
"	3/9/16	—	Inspected animal and standings of 24th, 72nd, & 38th Batty. R.F.A. of 6th Div. R.A.	
"	4/9/16	—	Inspected animal and standings of 6th Div. Ammn. Col.	
"	5/9/16	—	The Divisional Headquarters moved to ARBRE FOURCHE.	
ARBRE FOURCHE	6/9/16	—	The Divisional Headquarters moved from ARBRE FOURCHE to VILLA-DES-ETANGS near CORBIE. No 32 Mobile Veterinary Section moved from MEAULTE to VILLA-DES-ETANGS near CORBIE.	
CORBIE	7/9/16	—	Nothing to record.	
"	8/9/16	—	Inspected horses and standings of all Headquarters with the Division.	
"	9/9/16	—	Inspected horses and standings of No 32 Mobile Veterinary Section & the 11th K.R.R., 13th R.B.; and the S.A.A. Section of the 20th Div. Ammn. Col.	

WAR DIARY
or
INTELLIGENCE SUMMARY.
(Erase heading not required.)

Army Form C. 2118.

Instructions regarding War Diaries and Intelligence Summaries are contained in F. S. Regs., Part II. and the Staff Manual respectively. Title pages will be prepared in manuscript.

Place	Date	Hour	Summary of Events and Information	Remarks and references to Appendices
CORBIE	10/9/16		Inspected horses and standings of the whole of the 59th Infy. Bde.	
"	11/9/16		The Division moved from CORBIE to ARBRE FOURCHE shown on map 62d on L.2.b. The Mobile Veterinary Section moved from Villa de Etang near Corbie to MEAULTE. sheet 62d, E.17.c.5.1. Nothing to record.	
ARBRE FOURCHE	12/9/16		Inspected the horses and lines of 59th Infantry Bde, d.A.A. section of 20th Div. Ammn. Col., and No 32 Mobile Veterinary Section.	
"	13/9/16			
"	14/9/16		20th Div. R.A. rejoined the Division having marched by road from Ypres. Attended a conference of A.D.V.S of Fourth Army at the office of the D.D.V.S, Fourth Army.	
"	15/9/16		The Division stood to, ready to move, all the day.	
"	16/9/16		The day was occupied by collecting returns and forwarding the consolidated A.F.A.2000	
"	17/9/16		The Division moved into the line again. My office removed to the Citadel F.21.b.5.3. About midnight R.A.D.V.S. of Fourth Army at MEAULTE	
CITADEL	18/9/16		Attended a conference  to consider the establishing of a Vety. Casualty Clearing Station.	

WAR DIARY
or
INTELLIGENCE SUMMARY.
(Erase heading not required.)

Army Form C. 2118.

Place	Date	Hour	Summary of Events and Information	Remarks and references to Appendices
CITADEL	19/9/16		Nothing to record.	
"	20/9/16		Inspected horses and standings of 61, 2nd Infantry Bde, & the 83rd, 84th & 96th Field Coys R.E.	
"	21/9/16		The Divisional Headquarters moved to Folkd Tree Camp. L/C/b Albert Cooksted about.	
Folkd Tree Camp	22/9/16		The Divisional Headquarters moved to TREUX. Received checked A.F. A 2000	
TREUX	23/9/16		Rode to Bois des Taille, and arranged about the departure of Capt R.D. Williams, A.V.C. (T.F.) Inspected the animals of the Trench Mortar Batteries. Consolidated A.F.A 2000 sent in to D.D.V.S.	
"	24/9/16		The various charges were reallotted to the executive Vety Officers.	
"	25/9/16		Visited the Mob. Vety sect. at MEAULTE, the R.A. Headquarters at ARBRE FOURCHE and the 20th D.A.C. at Bois de Taille. Capt Williams A.V.C. (T.F) reported his departure for 47th Div.	
"	26/9/16		The D.D.V.S. Fourth Army called to inquire about A.V.C. dept. being posted in place of F.G.M.S.	
"	27/9/16		The Div. H.Q. moved forward and my Office moved to Folkd Tree Camp. L.2.b. Albert sheet.	

Army Form C. 2118.

WAR DIARY
or
INTELLIGENCE SUMMARY.
(Erase heading not required.)

Place	Date	Hour	Summary of Events and Information	Remarks and references to Appendices
ARBRE FOURCHE	28/9			
"	29/9		Visited the horses of No 4. Sect. 20th D.A.C., the Trench Mortar Batteries, & No 32 Mob. Vet. Sect. Visited the animals of all Headquarter units. Held a conference with the Veterinary Officers of the Division. Received A.F.s A2000	
"	30/9		for all units of the Division. Consolidated return for the week prepared and sent to the D.D.V.S., Fourth Army.	

30.9.16

T. Lithman,
Maj. A.V.C.,
A.D.V.S., 20th Division

Vol 5

A.D.V.S. 20th Division

October 1916

Army Form C. 2118.

WAR DIARY
or
INTELLIGENCE SUMMARY.
(Erase heading not required.)

Instructions regarding War Diaries and Intelligence Summaries are contained in F. S. Regs., Part II. and the Staff Manual respectively. Title pages will be prepared in manuscript.

Place	Date	Hour	Summary of Events and Information	Remarks and references to Appendices
ARBRE FOURCHE L2.b. Albert sheet (continued)	1/10/16		An Advanced Post from No. 32 Mob. Vety. Sect. was opened at A.13.d.0.2. Albert Bombined sheet, & had it published in Div. Orders. Visited Headquarters of 20th Div. Amm. Col.	
"	2/10/16		Kept an appointment to meet D.D.V.S. at MEAULTE	
"	3/10/16		Visited No. 2 Section 20th Div. Amm. Col., & E Batty. 91st Brigade R.F.A. to see about the transfer to the A.V.C. of two F.Q.M.S. Visited 158th Coy. A.S.C. nothing to record.	
"	4/10/16			
"	5/10/16		Inspected the horses & standing of the 158th, 159th, 160th & 161st Coys A.S.C. The 158th Coy are very good & the 161st only moderate. Visited No 32 Mob. Vety. Sect.	
"	6/10/16		My office removed from ARBRE FOURCHE to the CITADEL. Received the weekly returns from executive Veterinary Officers.	
CITADEL	7/10/16		Visited the advanced Dressing station at Bonroy & JB 32 Mob. Vety. Sect. in connection with the evacuation of cases coming in from other Divisions. Sent in to D.D.V.S., Fourth Army the consolidated weekly returns.	
"	8/10/16		Inspected the arrival of Div. Headquarters.	

Army Form C. 2118.

WAR DIARY
or
INTELLIGENCE SUMMARY.
(Erase heading not required.)

Instructions regarding War Diaries and Intelligence Summaries are contained in F. S. Regs., Part II. and the Staff Manual respectively. Title pages will be prepared in manuscript.

Place	Date	Hour	Summary of Events and Information	Remarks and references to Appendices
CITADEL	9/10/16	—	Div. Headquarters removed to TREUX.	
TREUX	10/10/16	—	Visited in my office by D.D.V.S., Fourth Army. Inspected 159 Bay A.O.S. & 96th Field Bay. R.E.	
"	11/10/16	—	Inspected the animals of the 59th Infantry Bde. Condition of all good; the 11th R.B. not quite so good.	
"	12/10/16	—	Inspected the animals of 60th & 61st Infantry Bde. & Field Bay. R.E.	
"	13/10/16	—	Inspected the Field Ambulance animals, sent in consolidated A.F. A. 2000	
"	14/11/16	—	Visited the Mob. Vety. Sect., & applied mallein test to the horses. Visited the Adjutant to the R.E., & 4 horses of 96th Fd. Bay. R.E. Handed over the Veterinary administration of 20th Div. R.A. to A.D.V.S. to Division.	
"	15/10/16	—	The Divisional Headquarters moved to Corbie. No reaction to mallein test. Passed 20th Div. R.A. under A.D.V.S., 6th Div.	
CORBIE	16/10/16	—	Visited Mobile Veterinary Section on arrival & billeted them at Villa de Etang.	
"	17/10/16	—	Attended at QUERRIEU a conference with D.D.V.S., Fourth Army.	
"	18/10/16	—	Nothing to record. The Division on the move. Pioneer Batt. & R.E. units passed under A.D.V.S. 8th Div.	

WAR DIARY
or
INTELLIGENCE SUMMARY.

(Erase heading not required.)

Army Form C. 2118.

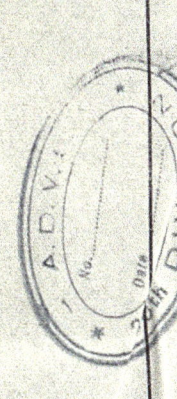

Place	Date	Hour	Summary of Events and Information	Remarks and references to Appendices
CORBIE	19/10/16		Moved from CORBIE to VIGNACOURT. Mobile Veterinary Section moved from VILLA-DES-ÉTANGS, CORBIE. to VIGNACOURT.	
VIGNACOURT	20/10/16		A.F. A.2000 received and consolidated returns made out and forwarded to D.D.V.S., FOURTH ARMY.	
"	21/10/16		Div. Headquarters and Mobile Veterinary Section moved from VIGNACOURT to BELLOY-SUR-SOMME.	
BELLOY	22/10/16		Inspected animals of 59th Infantry Bde.	
"	23/10/16		Inspected animals of 61st Infantry Bde; Machine Gun Coy; 161st Coy A.S.C.	
"	24/10/16		Nothing to record.	
"	25/10/16		Inspected all animals of Headquarters & 20th Fig. Coy.	
"	26/10/16		Inspected 59th Machine Gun Section. Inspected 60th Field Ambulance & 159 Coy A.S.C.	
"	27/10/16		Received return from V.O.s, and made out consolidated A.F.A.2000. Inspected animals and personnel of Mob.Vety. Sect.	
"	28/10/16		Inspected animals of 7th Batt. K.O.Y.L.I. and attended to office work awaiting disposal.	

Army Form C. 2118.

WAR DIARY
or
INTELLIGENCE SUMMARY.
(Erase heading not required.)

Instructions regarding War Diaries and Intelligence Summaries are contained in F. S. Regs., Part II. and the Staff Manual respectively. Title pages will be prepared in manuscript.

Place	Date	Hour	Summary of Events and Information	Remarks and references to Appendices
BELLOY.	29/10/16	—	Nothing to record.	
"	30/10/16	—	Visited N°32 Mob. Vety. Sect., 7th Batt. D.C.L.I., & 61st Machine Gun Company.	
"	31/10/16	—	Arranging fresh billets about 5 miles south of Belloy-en-Somme.	

T. Luthman,
Major A.V.C.,
A.D.V.S., 20th Div.

A.D.V.S.
31·10·16
20th DIVISION

Army Form C. 2118.

INTELLIGENCE SUMMARY

(Erase heading not required.)

Instructions regarding War Diaries and Intelligence Summaries are contained in F.S. Regs., Part II. and the Staff Manual respectively. Title Pages will be prepared in manuscript.

Place	Date	Hour	Summary of Events and Information	Remarks and references to Appendices
BELLOY	1/7/16		The Divisional Headquarters moved to Cavillon. Mobile Veterinary Section moved to BOISSY.	
CAVILLON	2/7/16		Visited 84th Field Coy. R.E. at FLIXECOURT.	
"	3/7/16		Visited 60th Field Ambulance and 159th Bgy. A.S.C at FOURDRINOY	
"	4/7/16		Visited 61st Field Ambulance near SOUES	
"	5/7/16		Visited Mobile Veterinary Section & afterwards accompanied D.D.R. Fourth Army to have horses purposed as remount cases.	
"	6/7/16		Engaged with Office work all day.	
"	7/7/16		Visited all the units of the 60th Brigade by motor.	
"	8/7/16		Had a conference of V.O.s to arrange the various changes.	
"	9/7/16		Visited the animals a line of 11th Batt. D.L.I., Headquarters of R.E. and 83rd Field Bgy. R.E.	
"	10/7/16		Visited 60th Field Ambulance, Capt Sellers A.V.C. proceeded on leave to England until 18·7·16.	
"	11/7/16		Visited 159 Bgy. A.S.C. and Mobile Veterinary Section	

2449 Wt. W14957/Mg0 750,000 1/16 J.B.C. & A. Forms/C.2118/12.

Army Form C. 2118.

WAR DIARY
or
INTELLIGENCE SUMMARY

(Erase heading not required.)

Instructions regarding War Diaries and Intelligence Summaries are contained in F. S. Regs., Part II. and the Staff Manual respectively. Title Pages will be prepared in manuscript.

Place	Date	Hour	Summary of Events and Information	Remarks and references to Appendices
CAVILLON	12/11/16	—	Making out consolidated return for the Division	
"	13/11/16	—	Nothing to record.	
"	14/11/16	—	Visited Mob. Vety. Sect. to arrange for Court Martial taking place this morning on Pte. Gilley & Knowles, A.V.C., turning to the non arrival of witnesses the Court Martial is postponed until 17.11.16	
"	15/11/16	—	The Divisional Headquarters removed to CORBIE. Mobile Veterinary Section to AILLY.	
CORBIE	16/11/16	—	Visited all Headquarter units. The Mobile Veterinary Section arrived in CORBIE.	
"	17/11/16	—	Took over Veterinary charge of the 60th Infty. Bde. Group during the absence of Capt. LeBlanc A.V.C.	
"	18/11/16	—	Consolidated A.F.A 2000 forwarded to D.D.V.S, Fourth Army.	
"	19/11/16	—	Visited 84th Field Coy R.E & 11th Batt. D.L.I.	
"	20/11/16	—	Visited all Units of 60th Infty Bde, 160 Coy A.S.C. & 11th D.L.I.	

WAR DIARY
or
INTELLIGENCE SUMMARY

Army Form C. 2118.

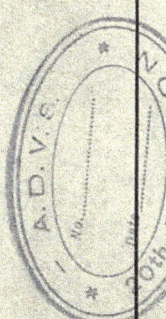

Place	Date	Hour	Summary of Events and Information	Remarks and references to Appendices
CORBIE	21/11/16		Visited the 12th K.R.R. & 6th Oxf & Bucks L.I. to see pack cobs that had been exchanged by 29th Division.	
"	22/11/16		Visited 84th Fld. Coy R.E. at DAOURS	
"	23/11/16		Visited Mt Headquarters units & Mobile Vety. Section. Capt. Sellen A.V.C. returned from leave.	
"	24/11/16		Visited the 59th Sty. Bde. at Méricourt, Treux & Ville-sur-Ancre to inspect pack cobs exchanged by 29th Division. Received weekly returns from Veterinary Officers. Consolidated returns sent to D.D.V.S. Fourth Army.	
"	25/11/16		Nothing to record. 91st Bde. R.F.A. arrived at Corbie.	
"	26/11/16		Inspected all the animals of 91st Brigade R.F.A. and N°/1 Section 20th D.A.C.	
"	27/11/16			
"	28/11/16		Visited Headquarters units & evacuated 22 horses from Corbie Station by A.D.V.S. Guards Division.	
"	29/11/16		Major J.B. Wellam A.V.C. of the M.V.S. proceeded on leave. Inspected 96th Field Coy. R.E. at DAOURS.	
"	30/11/16		Visited 91st Bde. R.F.A. & N°32 Mob. Vety. Sect.	

T. Lishman,
Maj. A.V.C.

WAR DIARY
or
INTELLIGENCE SUMMARY

Army Form C. 2118.

(Erase heading not required.)

Place	Date	Hour	Summary of Events and Information	Remarks and references to Appendices
CORBIE	1/12/16		Visited 161st Coy A.S.C., & 12th Kings Liverpools. Also No 72 Mobile Veterinary Section. Forwarded consolidated weekly return to D.D.V.S, Fourth Army	
"	2/12/16		Visited Lines of 60 Coy A.S.C. & 6th Batt. Dauphin L.I. Visited No 32 Mobile Veterinary Section	
"	3/12/16		Visited D.C.L.I. & K.S.L.I.	
"	4/12/16		Visited 12th K.R.R. & H.Q. of 60th Infantry Bde.	
"	5/12/16		Visited the Mobile Veterinary Section and 96th Field Coy. R.E.	
"	6/12/16		Nothing to record.	
"	7/12/16		Visited Mobile Veterinary Section & D.C.L.I. Transport Lines.	
"	8/12/16		Received the A.F.A 2000 for the Division from the V.Os.	
"	9/12/16		Consolidated A.F.A 2000 made out & sent to the D.D.V.S., Fourth Army.	
"	10/12/16		Visited Mob. Vety. Sect. & 96th Field Coy. R.E. at Daours.	
"	11/12/16		Nothing to record. Busy in Office concerning the Divn. return.	

WAR DIARY or INTELLIGENCE SUMMARY

Army Form C. 2118.

Place	Date	Hour	Summary of Events and Information	Remarks and references to Appendices
CORBIE	12/12/16	—	The Division moved up to the line. A.D.V.S. Office opened with Div. H.Q. (Rear) at A2.d.9.7. & N°32 M.V.S. moved to F.17.B.	
A2.d.9.7.	13/12/16	—	Visited Albert Combined. Inspected Headquarter Horses, 12th Batt. King's Liverpool, N°32 Mob. Vety. Sect, & 20th Div. Amm. Col.	
"	14/12/16	—	Visited 61st Machine Gun Coy, N°32 M.V.S., & 20th Div. Amm. Col.; Lt. I. Alexander, A.V.C. (T.C.) left the Div. for England on termination of agreement.	
"	15/12/16	—	Inspected the whole of 93rd Brigade R.F.A.	
"	16/12/16	—	Inspected the animals and standings of 83rd, 84th & 96th Field Coys. R.E.	
"	17/12/16	—	Inspected horses and standings of 60th, 61st & 62nd Field Ambulances	
"	18/12/16	—	Visited the Railhead at Plateau to arrange with the R.T.O. about the entraining of horses. Visited N°32 Mob. Vety. Sect.	
"	19/12/16	—	Visited A.D.V.S., 17th Division at Corbie to arrange relief.	
"	20/11/16	—	Inspected all Headquarter animals	

WAR DIARY
or
INTELLIGENCE SUMMARY
(Erase heading not required.)

Army Form C. 2118.

Place	Date	Hour	Summary of Events and Information	Remarks and references to Appendices
A.2.d.9.7.	21/12/16		Inspected the animals of 11th D.L.I., 59th & 60th Machine Gun Coys. Capt. G. Simm H.V.C. reported his arrival for duty from No. 1 Convalescent Horse Depôt.	
"	22/12/16		Received A.F.A. 2000 from V.Os. Visited the Div. Amm. Col. & 158 Coy. A.S.C.	
"	23/12/16		Attended a conference with D.D.V.S., Fourth Army. Visited Mobile Vety. Sect. Capt. Welham, returned from leave.	
"	24/12/16		Engaged in the Office all day.	
"	25/12/16		The Division moved into Reserve at Corbie.	
"	26/12/16		Visited 4th Army A.(H)T. Coy at Villers-sur-Ancre and inspected all the animals. 2 cases of mange found & had them evacuated. Notified the Town Major & had the billet marked.	
"	27/12/16		Visited 92nd Bde R.F.A. at Morlancourt & 6/91 & 6/92 Bde at Daours.	
"	28/12/16		Visited the whole of the 59th Infantry Bde Group and inspected their animals and lines.	
"	29/12/16		Received all A.F.A. 2000s for the Division.	

WAR DIARY
or
INTELLIGENCE SUMMARY

Army Form C. 2118.

Place	Date	Hour	Summary of Events and Information	Remarks and references to Appendices
CORBIE	30/12/16		Visited all Headquarters Units and Mob. Vety Sect.	
"	31/12/16		Capt. Welham having gone to collect a stray horse at Amiens, I took over charge of the M.V.S. and evacuated 20 horses to L. of C.	

31.12.16

T. Lithgow
Maj. A.V.C.
A.D.V.S., 20th Div.

WAR DIARY Vol 8
of the
A.D.V.S, 20th Division

January 1917.

Army Form C. 2118.

WAR DIARY
or
INTELLIGENCE SUMMARY

(Erase heading not required.)

Instructions regarding War Diaries and Intelligence Summaries are contained in F. S. Regs., Part II. and the Staff Manual respectively. Title Pages will be prepared in manuscript.

Place	Date	Hour	Summary of Events and Information	Remarks and references to Appendices
CORBIE	1/1/17	—	Visited 92nd Bde. R.F.A. at Morlancourt.	
"	2/1/17	—	Visited 6/91 & D 92 Batty. at DAOVRS. & Mob. Vety. Sect.	
"	3/1/17	—	Arranged move with A.D.V.S., Guards Division. Capt Bloy, A.V.C. proceeded to England on leave.	
"	4/1/17	—	Moved my office to Minden Post. Mob. Vety. Sect. moved to F.17.b.8.9. sheet Albert.	
Minden Post	5/1/17	—	Receiving return from V.Os. Visited Mob. Vety. Sect.	
"	6/1/17	—	Attended Conference with D.D.V.S., Fourth Army. Visited horses of 20th Signal Coy. at Dawn.	
"	7/1/17	—	nothing to record.	
"	8/1/17	—	At M.V.S. examining mange cases.	
"	9/1/17	—	Visited all units of 61st Infty. Bde, 61st Machine Gun Coy & 60th Machine Gun Coy.	
"	10/1/17	—	Visited the Div Hd Qtrs horse left at Corbie	

2449 Wt. W14957/M90 750,000 1/16 J.B.C. & A. Forms/C.2118/12.

Army Form C. 2118.

WAR DIARY
or
INTELLIGENCE SUMMARY

(Erase heading not required.)

Instructions regarding War Diaries and Intelligence Summaries are contained in F. S. Regs., Part II. and the Staff Manual respectively. Title Pages will be prepared in manuscript.

Place	Date	Hour	Summary of Events and Information	Remarks and references to Appendices
Minden Post	11/1/17	—	Visited 161 Coy A.S.C. & inspected for mange.	
"	12/1/17	—	Visited 'A' & 'B' Batty. 93rd Bde. R.F.A. & 20th Signal Coy at DAOURS.	
"	13/1/17	—	Handed over to Capt. W. Denington, A.V.C., & proceeded on leave.	
"	14/1/17	—	Nothing to record	
"	15/1/17	—	Visited 93. R.F.A. Bde. D. Batty. & inspected for mange	
"	16/1/17	—	Visited 161.Co A.S.C & inspected for mange.	
"	17/1/17	—	Nothing to record	
"	18/1/17	—	Visited Daours and inspected B.93. R.F.A. Bde. and Div. Signals	
"	19/1/17	—	Captain Clay. A.V.C. returned to Duty.	
"	20/1/17	—	Attended Conference with D.D.V.S. Fourth Army.	
"	21/1/17	—	Was informed water trough at Corery had been used by a mule having an outbreak of stomatitis. Had water trough disinfected.	
"	22/1/17	—	Visited M.V.S. amusement caves.	
"	23/1/17	—	Nothing to record	
"	24/1/17	—	Visited Daours & inspected for mange, no fresh suspected cases.	

WAR DIARY
or
INTELLIGENCE SUMMARY

Army Form C. 2118.

Place	Date	Hour	Summary of Events and Information	Remarks and references to Appendices
Morlancourt	25/1/17	—	Visited M.V.S. & Inspected Cases. Reorganized Veterinary charges for the Division whilst in Portrance. Maj. Lishman returned from leave.	
"	26/1/17	—	Visited No 2 Section 20th D.A.C. & No 32 Mob. Vety. Sect. Received A.F.A 2000.	
"	27/1/17	—	Mobile Veterinary Section moved to HEILLY. Consolidated return sent to D.D.V.S., Fourth Army.	
"	28/1/17	—	Divisional Headquarters moved to HEILLY.	
HEILLY	29/1/17	—	Inspected cases at M.V.S. & all horses of Headquarters, M.M.P., & 20th Sig. Coy.	
"	30/1/17	—	Inspected 'C' Batty. 93rd Bde. R.F.A. Hd.qrts. 91st & 93rd Bde. R.F.A. at Mulancourt.	
"	31/1/17	—	Attended Conference at the office of D.D.V.S., Fourth Army.	

31.1.17

T. Lishman,
Maj. A.V.C.
A.D.V.S., 20th Division

Vol 9

War Diary
of
A.D.V.S. 20th Divn
February 1917

Army Form C. 2118.

WAR DIARY
or
INTELLIGENCE SUMMARY

(Erase heading not required.)

Instructions regarding War Diaries and Intelligence Summaries are contained in F. S. Regs., Part II. and the Staff Manual respectively. Title Pages will be prepared in manuscript.

Place	Date	Hour	Summary of Events and Information	Remarks and references to Appendices
HEILLY	1/2/17		For personal information inspected cases of stomatitis in guards Division. Visited Mobile Veterinary Section.	
"	2/2/17		Visited Bonnay. Visited the 59th Infantry Bde. Group at Franvillers & inspected animals and transport lines of the following units: 96th Field Coy. R.E., 11th K.R.R.C., 159th Coy. A.S.C., 59th Machine Gun Coy., 60th Field Ambulance & 83rd Field Coy. R.E.	
"	3/2/17		Visited MEAULTE and inspected the animals & transport lines of the following units: 60th Infy Bde. H.Q., 6th Shropshire L.I., 6th Oxf. & Bucks L.I., 12th K.R.R.C., 12th R.B., 60th Machine Gun Coy., 11th D.L.I., 160th Coy. A.S.C. & 61st Field Ambulance.	
"	4/2/17		Nothing to record.	
"	5/2/17		Visited the 11th K.R.R. at Bonnay, and 12th King's Liverpool, & 7th K.O.Y.L.I. at LA NEUVILLE.	
"	6/2/17		Visited A/93 & B/93 Batty. R.F.A. and 20th Trig. Coy. at DAOURS.	
"	7/2/17		Visited all Headquarter animals.	
"	8/2/17		Nothing to record.	

WAR DIARY or INTELLIGENCE SUMMARY

Army Form C. 2118.

Place	Date	Hour	Summary of Events and Information	Remarks and references to Appendices
HEILLY	9/2/17	—	The Division moved to A.2.d.9.7. & N°32 M.V.S. to F.17.b. ref Albert (combined) sect.	
A.2.d.9.7.	10/2/17	—	Visited 91st & 92nd Bdes. R.F.A.	
"	11/2/17	—	Visited the Briquetorie.	
"	12/2/17	—	Visited N°2 section D.A.C. & N°32 Mob. Vety. Sect.	
"	13/2/17	—	Visited 93rd Bde R.F.A. at Morlancourt & 159, 160, & 161 Coys A.S.C.	
"	14/2/17	—	Visited M.V.S. in the morning & attend conference of D.D.V.S., Fourth Army.	
"	15/2/17	—	Visited Briquetorie, Mobile Vety. Sect. & 160 Coy. A.S.C.	
"	16/2/17	—	Visited 61st Field Ambulance & Mob. Vety. Sect.	
"	17/2/17	—	Visited 62nd Field Ambulance, 62nd M.G.C. & Mob. Vety. Sect. Consolidated return made out & sent to D.D.V.S.	
"	18/2/17	—	Mobile Vety. Sect & Headquarters Horses.	
"	19/2/17	—	Nothing to record.	

WAR DIARY
or
INTELLIGENCE SUMMARY

Army Form C. 2118.

Place	Date	Hour	Summary of Events and Information	Remarks and references to Appendices
A.2.d.9.7.	20/2/17	—	Nothing to record.	
"	21/2/17		Visited 59th Infantry Bde & Mob. Vety. Sect.	
"	22/2/17		Visited Brigade, 159, 160, & 161 Bde A.S.C. & Mob. Vety. Sect.	
"	23/2/17		Visited 60th Infantry Brigade & Mob. Vety. Sect.	
"	24/2/17		Visited 61st Infantry Bde & 83rd, 84th, & 96th Fld. Coys. R.E.	
"	25/2/17		Visited 60, 61 & 62nd Field Ambulances.	
"	26/2/17		Visited 158 Bry. A.S.C., & 'W' Battery R.H.A.	
"	27/2/17		Visited 20th Div. Amm. Col.	
"	28/2/17		Attended conference at the office of D.D.V.S., Fourth Army.	

T. Lithman
Maj. A.V.C.

Vol. 10

WAR DIARY.
OF
A.D.V.S. 20th Division.
MARCH 1917.

Army Form C. 2118.

WAR DIARY
or
INTELLIGENCE SUMMARY

(Erase heading not required.)

Instructions regarding War Diaries and Intelligence Summaries are contained in F. S. Regs., Part II. and the Staff Manual respectively. Title Pages will be prepared in manuscript.

Place	Date	Hour	Summary of Events and Information	Remarks and references to Appendices
A.2.d.9.7.	1/3/17	—	Inspected the horses and standings of the 4 Batteries of the 92nd Bde. R.F.A. Eight cases of debility were evacuated from "A" Batty.	
"	2/3/17	—	Inspected horses and standings of the 4 Batteries of the 91st Bde. R.F.A.	
"	3/3/17	—	Inspected animals & standings of 11th Batt. D.L.I. (Pioneers), and sent the consolidated A.F.A. 2000 to D.D.V.S., Fourth Army.	
"	4/3/17	—	Visited the horses of advanced D.H.Q., 159, 160 & 161 Coy. A.S.C., & No. 32 M.V.S.	
"	5/3/17	—	Mobile Veterinary Section, & accumulated office work.	
"	6/3/17	—	Inspected 158 Coy. A.S.C., & visited M.V.S.	
"	7/3/17	—	Inspected horses & stables of D.H.Q., visited M.V.S., & checking Vety. equipment	
"	8/3/17	—	Inspected the animals of 61st Infantry Brigade & visited M.V.S.	
"	9/3/17	—	Inspected animals & standings of 159, 160 & 161 Coy. A.S.C. & examined 6 cases of mange. Visited 60th & 61st Field Ambulances Advanced section of 20th D.A.C.	
"	10/3/17	—	Was present at Plateau Railhead to see entrainment of sick animals, visited Mobile Vety. Sect & 159, 160 & 161 Coy. A.S.C.	

WAR DIARY or INTELLIGENCE SUMMARY

Army Form C. 2118.

Place	Date	Hour	Summary of Events and Information	Remarks and references to Appendices
A.2.d.9.7.	11/3/17		Visited 159, 160, & 161 Regt. A.S.C. & 61st Machine Gun Company.	
"	12/3/17		" " " " " & Mobile Veterinary Section.	
"	13/3/17		" " " " ", Mobile Vety. Sect., Railhead to see the entrainment of sick animals, and Divl. Hd'qts. at Brignolaise	
"	14/3/17		Visited 60th Infty. Bde & Machine Gun Coy. & 20th Division Train	
"	15/3/17		" 59th " " " & " & Mobile Vety. Sect.	
"	16/3/17		Visited 61st Infantry Bde Machine Gun Coy.	
"	17/3/17		Visited 92nd Bde. R.F.A. & 20th Divn Train.	
"	18/3/17		Inspected all animals of Divn. Hd'Qts. Visited Mob. Vety. Sect.	
"	19/3/17		Divisional Rear Headquarters moved to Brignolaise (A.4.d.5.2.)	
A.4.d.5.2.	20/3/17		Engaged in the office all day & visited 20th Divn Train.	
"	21/3/17		No. 32 Mob. Vety. Sect. moved from Minden Post to Brignolaise.	

Army Form C. 2118.

WAR DIARY
or
INTELLIGENCE SUMMARY

(Erase heading not required.)

Instructions regarding War Diaries and Intelligence Summaries are contained in F. S. Regs., Part II. and the Staff Manual respectively. Title Pages will be prepared in manuscript.

Place	Date	Hour	Summary of Events and Information	Remarks and references to Appendices
A.4.d.5.2.	22/3/17		Visited 59th Infty. Bde., 20th Signal Coy, Mob. Vety. Sect., & 20th Div. Train.	
"	23/3/17		Received A.F.s A 2000 from Vety. Officers. Visited 11th Batt. D.L.I. & M.V.S.	
"	24/3/17		Evacuating horse from M.V.S., Visited 61st Machine gun Coy, 217th M.G.C. arrived from England.	
"	25/3/17		Visited 20th Div. Train, Mob. Vety. Sect., and arranged with 217th M.G.C. for the malleining of their animals.	
"	26/3/17		Engaged with office work.	
"	27/3/17		Visited 62nd Field Ambulance & malleined the 54 animals of 217 M.G.C.	
"	28/3/17		Visited 158 Coy. A.S.C. 83, 84 & 96th Field Coy R.E., & 60th & 61st Field Ambulance also the 217th Machine gun Coy - all had given negative reaction to mallein. Visited M.V.S., 20th Signal Coy, Headquarters Horse & 158 Coy A.S.C.	
"	29/3/17		Received A.F. A2000 from V.Os, visited 159, 160 & 161 Coys. A.S.C.	
"	30/3/17		Engaged with the consolidated weekly return, sent in a weekly summary on the Vety. administration of the Division to D.D.V.S., First Army.	
"	31/3/17			

T. Lishman,
Major, A.V.C.,
A.D.V.S., 20th Division

War Diary Vol XI
A.D.V.S., 20 Division
April 1917

Army Form C. 2118.

WAR DIARY
or
INTELLIGENCE SUMMARY
(Erase heading not required.)

Instructions regarding War Diaries and Intelligence Summaries are contained in F. S. Regs., Part II. and the Staff Manual respectively. Title Pages will be prepared in manuscript.

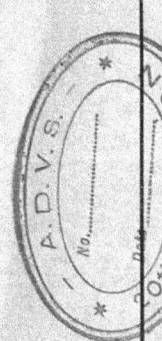

Place	Date	Hour	Summary of Events and Information	Remarks and references to Appendices
A.4.d.5.2. Sheet Albert (continued)	1/4/17	—	Nothing to record.	
"	2/4/17	—	Rode to Le Transloy to select a site for No 32 M.V.S. An enemy aeroplane dropped a bomb at base station killing 17 animals of 59th Infantry Bde. Headquarters.	
"	3/4/17	—	The Divisional rear H.Q. moved forward to ROCQUIGNY. Inspected the animals of 20th Div. Train.	
ROCQUIGNY	4/4/17	—	Inspected the animals of S.A.A. Section D.A.C. & reported to G.O.C. that their condition was good. Recommended not more than 75% of available animals to be detailed for daily duty. No 32 Mobile Veterinary Section moved to LE TRANSLOY.	
"	5/4/17	—	Visited 60th Field Ambulance, Mobile Vety. Sect., 11th D.I.I., & 20th Fig. Coy.	
"	6/4/17	—	Visited & inspected all the animals & lines of the 91st Bde. R.F.A. Weekly A.F.A 2000 despatched to D.D.V.S. Fourth Army.	
"	7/4/17	—	Inspected all the animals & standing of the 92nd Bde. R.F.A.	
"	8/4/17	—	Inspected 62nd Field Amb., 96th Field Coy R.E. & Mob. Vety. Sect.	
"	9/4/17	—	Inspected 59th Infantry Bde., 59th M.G. Coy & visited 96th Fld. Coy.	

Army Form C. 2118.

WAR DIARY
or
INTELLIGENCE SUMMARY
(Erase heading not required.)

Place	Date	Hour	Summary of Events and Information	Remarks and references to Appendices
ROCQUIGNY	10/4/17	—	Inspected 62nd Fld. Ambulance, Horses of Div. H.Q. & 20th Sig. Coy.	
"	11/4/17	—	Inspected 60th Infantry Bde. & visited M.V.S.	
"	12/4/17	—	Inspected 61st Infty. Bde.	
"	13/4/17	—	Inspected 61st M.G.Co., visited 96th Fld. Coy. R.E.; Consolidated A.F.A 2000 forwarded to D.D.V.S.	
"	14/4/17	—	Visited 61st Infantry Bde & 159 Coy A.S.C. & visited M.V.S.	
"	15/4/17	—	Visited 20th Sig. Coy. & M.M.P.	
"	16/4/17	—	Inspected 83rd & 84th Field Coys. R.E., 12th Kings hinderquarters and Mob. Vety. Sect.	
"	17/4/17	—	Inspected 217th M.G.C. & 7th Batt. Somerset L.I. & visited M.V.S.	
"	18/4/17	—	Inspected 61st Machine Gun Coy., & 60th Field Ambulance at Moislans.	
"	19/4/17	—	Inspected 61 & 62 Field Ambulances & 11th Batt. D.L.I.	
"	20/4/17	—	Inspected 60th Infantry Brigade & visited Mob. Vety. Sect.	

Army Form C. 2118.

WAR DIARY
or
INTELLIGENCE SUMMARY

(Erase heading not required.)

Instructions regarding War Diaries and Intelligence Summaries are contained in F. S. Regs., Part II. and the Staff Manual respectively. Title Pages will be prepared in manuscript.

Place	Date	Hour	Summary of Events and Information	Remarks and references to Appendices
ROCQUIGNY	21/4/17	—	Inspected 158 & 160 Coys A.S.C.; 96th Field Coy R.E. & forwarded consolidated return to D.D.V.S. & visited M.V.S.	
"	22/4/17	—	Inspected 159 & 161 Coys A.S.C. & visited M.V.S.	
"	23/4/17	—	Inspected 59th Infantry Bde & Machine Gun Company.	
"	24/4/17	—	Inspected the whole of the 20th Divn. Amm. Col.	
"	25/4/17	—	Visited Mob. Vety. Sect. & attended to surplus office work.	
"	26/4/17	—	Inspected 'A' & 'E' Batty, 92nd Bde R.F.A. & visited the A.D.V.S. for the purpose of seeing the Divn. Horse Rest Station.	
"	27/4/17	—	Inspected 'B' & 'D' Batty, 92nd Bde. R.F.A.; Mob. Vety. Section moved to ROCQUIGNY. Sent consolidated return to D.D.V.S.	
"	28/4/17	—	Inspected 'A' C & 'D' Batty 91st Brigade R.F.A.	
"	29/4/17	—	'B' Batty 91st Bde R.F.A., A.A.A. Section 20th D.A.C. and visited Mob. Vety. Sect.	
"	30/4/17	—	My office moved to YTRES (P.26.b.5.0. Sheet 57 C 1:40,000) Visited Headquarters Units & main watering point.	

T. Lehmann,
Maj. A.V.C.

Vol 12

WAR DIARY
MAY 1917
A.D.V.S. 20th Division

Army Form C. 2118.

WAR DIARY
or
INTELLIGENCE SUMMARY

(Erase heading not required.)

Instructions regarding War Diaries and Intelligence Summaries are contained in F. S. Regs., Part II. and the Staff Manual respectively. Title Pages will be prepared in manuscript.

Place	Date	Hour	Summary of Events and Information	Remarks and references to Appendices
YPRES (P.26.b.5.0.) 57cNL4.0,0002	1/5/17		Visited 61st Infantry Bde, 61st M.G.C, & 60th Rifle.	
"	2/5/17		Visited 11th R.B., 96th Field Coy, 61st Field Ambulance. Mob. Vety. Section & Regrouping R.B. Llhead.	
"	3/5/17		Attended 2nd D.V.S. Conference at Villers Faucomet. Visited 83rd Field Coy R.E., Mob. Vety. Sect, & Div. H'qrs.	
"	4/5/17		Visited 62nd Field Ambulance, 61st M.G.C., Mob. Vety. Sect. 84th Field Coy R.E. Made arrangements for demonstration of anti-gas measures for horses.	
"	5/5/17		Visited 20th Signal Coy., 11th D.L.I. & Mob. Vety. Sect	
"	6/5/17		Visited 20th Div. H'qrs., Anti-gas demonstration to all A.V.C. personnel of Division.	
"	7/5/17		Visited 60th Infty. Bde., 21st M.G.C., Anti-gas demonstration to A.V.C. personnel continued.	
"	8/5/17		"	
"	9/5/17		Nothing to record. Office work	
"	10/5/17		"	

Army Form C. 2118.

WAR DIARY
or
INTELLIGENCE SUMMARY
(Erase heading not required.)

Instructions regarding War Diaries and Intelligence Summaries are contained in F. S. Regs., Part II. and the Staff Manual respectively. Title Pages will be prepared in manuscript.

Place	Date	Hour	Summary of Events and Information	Remarks and references to Appendices
YPRES	11/5/17	—	Inspected 158, 159, 160, & 161 Bttys A.F.A. & Army wilt consolidated A.F.A. 2000.	
"	12/5/17	—	Inspected 59th Infantry Bde.	
"	13/5/17	—	Visited M.V.S., & 158 Bty A.F.A., Inspected 10 D.A.C. mules attached to 59th Infantry Bde. Headquarters for special report. 2.D.V.S., Fourth Army visited the Division & inspected two Batteries of R.F.A., No 1 & 2 sections of the 20th Div. Amm. Col., "61st Infantry Bde, & 158 Bty A.F.A. Div. H.Q. 3th Horse, 20th Signal Coy.	
"	14/5/17	—	Looked over the horses of 91st & 92nd Bde. R.F.A.	
"	15/5/17	—	Visited Mobile Veterinary Section, engaged in evacuating debilitated animals from all units in the Div.	
"	16/5/17	—	Inspected 91st Bde. R.F.A.	
"	17/5/17	—	Inspected 20th Div Ammn. Col.	
"	18/5/17	—	Inspected 92nd Bde. R.F.A.	
"	19/5/17	—	Visited the A.D.V.S. 5th Australian Division & arrange of almost taking over his area on relief of the Division by the 20th Div.	

WAR DIARY
or
INTELLIGENCE SUMMARY

(Erase heading not required.)

Army Form C. 2118.

Place	Date	Hour	Summary of Events and Information	Remarks and references to Appendices
YPRES	20/5/17		Inspected the arrival of the 61st Infantry Bde.	
"	21/5/17		" " " 59th " "	
"	22/5/17		" " " 96th Field Coy. R.E., & 2nd Field	
"	23/5/17		Ambulance. Visited M.V.S. 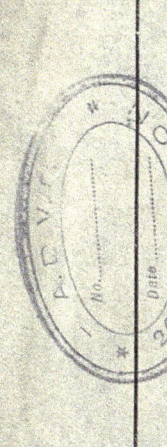 Office move to H.15.C. (The "Monument", nr Bapaume)	
Th. Monument	24/5/17		No 32 M.V.S. moved to H.21.a. (Reference sheet 57c) Inspected the arrival of the 59th & 60th Infantry Brigades, & 96th Field Coy. R.E.	
"	25/5/17		Visited 83rd & 84th Field Coy. R.E., 20th Signal Coy, 60th & 61st Field Ambulance, both in consolidated A.F.A. 2000 to D.D.V.S. Fifth Army.	
"	26/5/17		Inspected the 60th Infantry Bde.	
"	27/5/17		Inspected the 11th Batt. D.L.I. & the 60th & 217th M.G. Coy.	
"	28/5/17		Maj. Littman, A.D.V.S., proceeded on 10 days leave to England. Capt. W. Derrington, A.V.C. acting A.D.V.S.	

Army Form C. 2118.

WAR DIARY
or
INTELLIGENCE SUMMARY
(Erase heading not required.)

Instructions regarding War Diaries and Intelligence Summaries are contained in F. S. Regs., Part II. and the Staff Manual respectively. Title Pages will be prepared in manuscript.

Place	Date	Hour	Summary of Events and Information	Remarks and references to Appendices
The Monument	29/5/17	—	Nothing to record	
"	30/5/17	—	Inspected all units	
	31/5/17		Making arrangements for moving M.V.S.	

W. Dening Lt. Capt A.V.C.
for A.D.V.S.
20th Division

[Stamp: A.D.V.S. 20th DIVISION]

2449 Wt. W14957/M90 750,000 1/16 J.B.C. & A. Forms/C.2118/12.

WAR DIARY OF ADVS 20th DIVN

JUNE 1917

Army Form C. 2118.

WAR DIARY
or
INTELLIGENCE SUMMARY

(Erase heading not required.)

Instructions regarding War Diaries and Intelligence Summaries are contained in F. S. Regs, Part II. and the Staff Manual respectively. Title Pages will be prepared in manuscript.

Place	Date	Hour	Summary of Events and Information	Remarks and references to Appendices
The MONUMENT H.15.C.	1/6/17		Nº 32 M.V.S. moved to H.21.c.2.2. sheet 57c Consolidated A.F. A.2000 sent to D.D.V.S., Third Army. Inspected 61st Infantry Bde.	
"	2/6/17		Inspected 61st Infantry Bde.	
"	3/6/17		" 83rd, 84th, & 96th Field Coy. R.E.	
"	4/6/17		" 59th & 60th Infantry Bde. Nº 32 M.V.S. moved to H.16.d.2.2. sheet 57c	
"	5/6/17		Inspected 20th Signal Coy., R.A. Headquarters, 92nd Bde. R.F.A. Nºs 1 & 2 A Hd.Qrs, 20th D.A.C. Also 159, 160, & 161 Coy A.S.C.	
"	6/6/17		Inspected 91st Bde. R.F.A., 158 Coy. A.S.C., Nº 3 sect. D.A.C., & 20th Div. H.Q.	
"	7/6/17		Nothing to record.	
"	8/6/17		Made out & forwarded to D.D.V.S., Third Army Consolidated A.F.A 2000	
"	9/6/17		Major T. Lihman, A.D.V.S., returned from leave.	
"	10/6/17		Nothing to record.	

Army Form C. 2118.

WAR DIARY
or
INTELLIGENCE SUMMARY

(Erase heading not required.)

Instructions regarding War Diaries and Intelligence Summaries are contained in F. S. Regs., Part II. and the Staff Manual respectively. Title Pages will be prepared in manuscript.

Place	Date	Hour	Summary of Events and Information	Remarks and references to Appendices
"	11/6/17		Visited No 32 Mob. Vety. Sect., 60th & 61st & 62nd Field Ambulance, Capt. J.B. Wellcome, A.V.C., V.O., No 32 M.V.S. went to Paris, 10 days leave.	
"	12/6/17		Office work.	
"	13/6/17		Visited 158, 159, 160, & 161 Coys. A.S.C. to examine skin cases, & administered 60th & 62nd Field Ambulance	
"	14/6/17		Visited 61st Field Ambulance, 83rd & 96th Field Coys. R.E., 217th Machine Gun Coy. & 11th Batt. D.L.I.	
"	15/6/17		Visited 84th Field Coy. R.E. & Mob. Vety. Sect.	
"	16/6/17		Visited all Coys. of Div. Train & Mob. Vety. Sect.	
"	17/6/17		Busy at the Mob. Vety. Sect. Office.	
"	18/6/17		Visited 12th Kings Liverpool, 62nd Field Ambulance, and Mob. Vety. Sect.	
"	19/6/17		Visited 'A','B','C', & 'D' Battys. 91st Bde. R.F.A. & Bde. Hd Qrts.	
"	20/6/17		Visited 'A','B','C', & 'D' Battys. 92nd Bde. R.F.A. & Bde. Hd Qrts.	

WAR DIARY
or
INTELLIGENCE SUMMARY

(Erase heading not required.)

Army Form C. 2118.

Place	Date	Hour	Summary of Events and Information	Remarks and references to Appendices
"	21/6/17	—	Visited Nos 2 & 3 Section of 20th D.A.C., & No 3 Section in the evening.	
"	22/6/17	—	Visited 59th Infantry Bde., 61st Machine Gun Coy & M.V.S.	
"	23/6/17	—	Consolidated A.F.A. 2000 forwarded to 2D.V.S., Third Army & allotted changes for new area.	
"	24/6/17	—	Visited 11th Batt. D.L.I. 59th & 60th M.G.C., 83rd Field Coy. R.E. and showed the A.D.V.S. of 62nd Division his new area & arranged to moving of M.V. Sections.	
"	25th	—	Visited 60th Infantry Bde and Mob.Vety.Sect.	
"	26th	—	Visited 61st Infantry Bde. and Mob.Vety.Sect	
"	27th	—	Visited the 61st Infantry Bde and Mob.Vet.Sect. again.	
"	28th	—	Moved my office to BERNAVILLE, W.S.W. of DOULLENS.	
"	29th	—	No 32 Mobile Veterinary Section moved to ACHEUX, from " to BERNAVILLE.	
"	30	—	" " " to BERNAVILLE	

T. Lihman
Maj. A.V.C.
A.D.V.S. 20th Div.

Vol 14

Alan Strand
DADVS
July 1917

Army Form C. 2118.

WAR DIARY
or
INTELLIGENCE SUMMARY

(Erase heading not required.)

D.A.D.V.S.
20TH DIVISION.

Place	Date	Hour	Summary of Events and Information	Remarks and references to Appendices
BERNAVILLE	1/7/17		Moved my Office to DOMART-EN-PONTHIEU. Received information from D.V.S. that an A.D.V.S. had been appointed to Corps, A.D.V.S. of Division would become D.A.D.V.S.	
"	2/7/17		Inspected 10th K.R.R., 10th R.B., & 11th D.L.I.	
"	3/7/17		Inspected 84 & 96th Field Coys, 59th Infty Bde. Hd Qrtrs M.G. Co., 11th K.R.R. & 11th R.B., 159 Coy A.S.C. & 60th Field Ambulance	
"	4/7/17		Inspected 60th Infantry Bde. Hd Qrtrs, 6th Ox & Bucks L.I., 6th K.S.L.I., 12th K.R.R., & 12th R.B.	
"	5/7/17		Inspected 60th M.G. Co., 61st Field Ambulance, 8160 Coy A.S.C.	
"	6/7/17		Office work on return. Consolidated A.F.A. 2000 forwarded A.D.V.S., IVth Corps. Visited No 32 Mob. Vety. Sect.	
"	7/7/17		Inspected 12th Kings Liverpool, 7th D.C.L.I., & 161 Coy. A.S.C.	
"	8/7/17		Inspected 61st M.G. Co., 61st Infty. Bde Hd Qrtrs, 7 Somerset L.I. & 7th K.O.Y.L.I.	

WAR DIARY or INTELLIGENCE SUMMARY

Army Form C. 2118.

D.A.D.V.S.
20TH DIVISION.

Place	Date	Hour	Summary of Events and Information	Remarks and references to Appendices
DOMART	9/7/17	—	Inspected 217th M.G.C., & 62nd Field Ambulance.	
"	10/7/17	—	" 83rd Field Coy., 20th Signal Coy. & Divisional Hd'Qtrs.	
"	11/7/17	—	Inspected 60th & 61st Fld. Ambulances & visited M.V.S.	
"	12/7/17	—	Visited 159 Coy A.S.C., 10th R.B., 11th R.B.	
"	13/7/17	—	Engaged in the Office with returns & visited M.V.S.	
"	14/7/17	—	Visited 11th K.R.R. & 11th R.B.	
"	15/7/17	—	No T/7/02605 Staff Sergt. McKAY, P., A.V.C. reported his arrival at No 32 M.V.S.	
"	16/7/17	—	Visited 12th Kings, 7th Somersets & 7th D.C.L.I., A M.V.S.	
"	17/7/17	—	" 60th Bde Hd'Qtrs, & 61st M.G.C., K.O.Y.L.I., 61st Infy. Bde Hd'Qtrs, & 61st M.G.C.	
"	18/7/17	—	Nothing to record. Visited M.V.S.	
"	19/7/17	—	Issued orders regarding the entrainment of animals for the Divisional Horse Show	

WAR DIARY
or
INTELLIGENCE SUMMARY

(Erase heading not required.)

Army Form C. 2118.

D.A.D.V.S.,
20TH DIVISION.

Place	Date	Hour	Summary of Events and Information	Remarks and references to Appendices
DOMART	20/7/17		The Division commenced entraining for PROVEN area.	
"	21/7/17		The Division completed its move & opened at PROVEN.	
PROVEN	22/7/17		Visited the A.D.V.S., XIVth Corps. A reported arrival of Mob. Vety. Sect. situated in PROVEN.	
"	23/7/17		Inspected 20th D.A.C. in connection with 15 cases of ringworm to Divisional Train. A.D.V.S. XIV th Corps.	
"	24/7/17		Inspected 20th Divisional Train. Inspected No. 32 M.V.S.	
"	25/7/17		Nothing to record.	
"	26/7/17		Visited whole of 60th Infantry Bde group.	
"	27/7/17		Received return from V.O.	
"	28/7/17		Attended Conference at office of A.D.V.S.	
"	29/7/17		Visited M.V.S., Corps M.V.S. & D.A.D.V.S., 29th Division	
"	30/7/17		Inspected 61st Infantry Bde., 2/61 Coy. A.S.C.	
"	31/7/17		Inspected animals of 158 Coy. A.S.C. and visited the forward area where the 20th Div. R.A. Horse had moved to - 2 miles N. of Brielen.	

T. Lidman
Maj. A.V.C.

Army Form C. 2118.

D.A.D.V.S.
20TH DIVISION.
No. ....
Date ....

Vol/5

WAR DIARY
or
INTELLIGENCE SUMMARY
(Erase heading not required.)

Instructions regarding War Diaries and Intelligence Summaries are contained in F. S. Regs., Part II. and the Staff Manual respectively. Title Pages will be prepared in manuscript.

Place	Date	Hour	Summary of Events and Information	Remarks and references to Appendices
Dragon Camp	7/8/17	—	Inspected 59th M.G.C., 10th K.R.R., 217th M.G.C., 11th Batt. D.L.I., 60th Field Ambulance; & 93rd Bde. R.F.A. Casualties = 1 destroyed	
"	8/8/17		Inspected 59th Infy. Bde. Hd'Qrtrs, 10th Batt. R.B., 11th K.R.R., 11th R.B. & 159 Bde. A.S.C. Casualties 1 killed, 1 destroyed & 12 wounded.	
"	9/8/17		Inspected 91st & 92nd Bde. R.F.A. Casualties = 5 wounded.	
"	10/8/17		Captn. A.J. Sellars, A.V.C. (T.C.) left the Division. Inspected 20th Divn Ammn. Col. Casualties = 7 killed, 16 wounded.	
"	11/8/17		Attended Conference of A.D.V.S., XIVth Corps Casualties = 6 killed, & 23 wounded.	
"	12/8/17		Inspected 20th Signal Coy., 158 Bde.A.S.C., 160 Coy A.S.C. Casualties = 10 killed & 13 wounded.	
"	13/8/17		Inspected 62nd Field Ambulance Casualties = 3 wounded	
"	14/8/17		Visited the 20th Division Royal Artillery with Horse Adviser XIVth Corps. Casualties = 8 killed, 1 destroyed & 4 wounded.	

Army Form C. 2118.

WAR DIARY
or
INTELLIGENCE SUMMARY

(Erase heading not required.)

D.A.D.V.S.,
20TH DIVISION.

No. ....
Date ....

Instructions regarding War Diaries and Intelligence Summaries are contained in F. S. Regs., Part II. and the Staff Manual respectively. Title Pages will be prepared in manuscript.

Place	Date	Hour	Summary of Events and Information	Remarks and references to Appendices
DRAGON CAMP	15/8/17	—	Inspected 161 Coy. A.S.C. Casualties = 2 Killed, 2 destroyed, 8 wounded.	
"	16/8/17	—	Inspected 83rd, 84th & 96th Field Coys. R.E. Casualties = 2 wounded.	
"	17/8/17	—	Consolidating A.F.A 2000 for the Division. Casualties = 15 wounded.	
"	18/8/17	—	Attended Conference of A.D.V.S., XIVth Corps. Casualties = 7 wounded.	
"	19/8/17	—	Office & M.V.S. moved to PROVEN. Casualties = 6 wounded.	
PROVEN	20/8/17	—	Visited the Hergele–Hirthoepe area in connexion with the 20th Div. R.A. Battery outretreat. Casualties = 1 wounded.	
"	21/8/17	—	Inspected the 60th Infantry Bde., 60th M.G.C., 217th M.G.C., 61st Field Ambulance. Casualties = 2 wounded.	
"	22/8/17	—	Inspected 61st Infantry Bde & 61st M.G.C. " " & 59th "	
"	23/8/17	—	" 59th " " " "	

Army Form C. 2118.

WAR DIARY
or
INTELLIGENCE SUMMARY

(Erase heading not required.)

Instructions regarding War Diaries and Intelligence Summaries are contained in F. S. Regs., Part II. and the Staff Manual respectively. Title Pages will be prepared in manuscript.

Place	Date	Hour	Summary of Events and Information	Remarks and references to Appendices
PROVEN	24/8/17		Consolidated A.F.A. 2000 compiled.	
"	25/8/17		Attended Conference with A.D.V.S., XIVth Corps.	
"	26/8/17		Took over the 59th & 61st Infantry Bde. Group from Capt. W. Denington A.V.C. proceeding on leave.	
"	27/8/17		Capt. Denington went on 10 days leave to England. Visited 61st Infantry Bde.	
"	28/8/17		Visited 59th Infantry Bde. & Mob. Vety. Sect.	
"	29/8/17		Visited 61st Infantry Bde. & " " "	
"	30/8/17		" 59th " "	
"	31/8/17		" 61st " "	

T. Lishman
Maj. A.V.C.

D.A.D.V.S.
20TH DIVISION.
No.
Date 1.9.17

Army Form C. 2118.

WAR DIARY
or
INTELLIGENCE SUMMARY
(Erase heading not required.)

D.A.D.V.S.
20TH DIVISION.

Vol/6

Place	Date	Hour	Summary of Events and Information	Remarks and references to Appendices
PROVEN	1/9/17		Attended the conference of the A.D.V.S., XIVth Corps & took the consolidated A.F.A 2000 Visited 59th Infantry Bde. Group.	
"	2 "		Inspected the D.L.I. & 160th Coy. A.S.C. Visited 61st Infty. Bde. Group.	
"	3 "		O.C., No. 32 M.V.S. took over charge of XIVth Corps M.V.S. & the M.V.S. moved to the site of the latter at E.12.d.what.27	
"	4 "		Visited 61st Infantry Bde. Group.	
"	5 "		" 59th " "	
"	6 "		" 61st " "	
"	7 "		O.C. 32 M.V.S. relinquished charge of Corps M.V.D.S. & the M.V.S. returned to E.18.b.1.1. sheet 27 Visited 59th Infantry Bde. Group. Received weekly return from V.O.s	
"	8 "		Attended A.D.V.S., weekly conference & took consolidated A.F.A 2000 Capt. Donnington returned from leave & took over 59 & 61st Infty. Bde. Visited 20th Divisional Train. Capt G. Simmers proceeded to England on 10 days leave	
"	9 "		Visited new area & M.V.S. Office work.	
"	10 "			

Army Form C. 2118.

WAR DIARY
or
INTELLIGENCE SUMMARY

(Erase heading not required.)

D.A.D.V.S., 20TH DIVISION.

Place	Date	Hour	Summary of Events and Information	Remarks and references to Appendices
PROVEN	11/9/17	—	Office moved to Welsh Farm (B.14.c.15.15. Sheet 28), N° 32 Mobile Veterinary Section moved to A.9.c.7.3. & Advanced Veterinary Aid Post to B.20.a.5.3. both reference sheet 28. 7 Horses wounded.	
Welsh Farm	12/9/17	—	Visited 20th Div. Ammn. Col. & N° 1 Sect. 29th D.A.C. the inquire into casualties — 46 animals killed & 42 wounded. Report sent to A.D.V.S.	
"	13/9/17	—	Visited 91st & 92nd Bdes. R.F.A.	
"	14/9/17	—	Visited, inspected & reported to Q. on 59th Infty. Bde. & M.G.C., 60th Infty. Bde. & M.G.C., & 61st Bde. & M.G.C., & 217th M.G.C.; Received a return from V.Os. Is of which	
"	15/9/17	—	Attended weekly Conference at office of A.D.V.S. XIVth Corps & took consolidated A.F.A 2000 to 'Q'. the 83rd, 84th & 96th	
"	16/9/17	—	Visited, inspected & reported on to 'Q' the Hd'Qrters & 60th Field Ambulance. Field Coys. R.E., 59th Infty. Bde. Hd'Qrters & 60th Field Ambulance.	
"	17/9/17	—	Visited, inspected & reported on to 'Q', 20th Signal Coy, 61st M.G.C., 11th D.L.I. & 61st Field Ambulance.	

Army Form C. 2118.

WAR DIARY
or
INTELLIGENCE SUMMARY

(Erase heading not required.)

D.A.D.V.S.,
20TH DIVISION.

Instructions regarding War Diaries and Intelligence Summaries are contained in F.S. Regs., Part II. and the Staff Manual respectively. Title Pages will be prepared in manuscript.

Place	Date	Hour	Summary of Events and Information	Remarks and references to Appendices
Walsh Farm	18/9/17	—	Visited, inspected & reported to 'Q' on 20th Gen; Train.	
"	19/9/17	—	The A.D.V.S., XIVth Corps inspected the whole of the animals of the 20th Division (less R.A.)	
"	20/9/17	—	Visited the 91st & 92nd Bdes. R.F.A. & reported to C.R.A. that general condition were good with the exception of a few thin animals in each Battery.	
"	21/9/17	—	Visited Mobile Vety. Sect. & received return from the V.O.s visited D.C.L.I. in connexion with the trials of injections of Lugols solution for Ophthalmia.	
"	22/9/17	—	Attended Conference at Office of A.D.V.S., XIVth Corps, & took Consolidated A.F.A. 2000. Visited M.V.S.	
"	23/9/17	—	Visited 60th Infantry Bde. & M.G.C., 7th D.C.L.I. & 7th Somerset L.I. Gave demonstration of injecting Lugols solution in the treatment of Ophthalmia in the D.C.L.I. Lines. Went around the area.	
"	24/9/17	—	Visited M.V.S.	
"	25/9/17	—	Visited the D.A.D.V.S. 4th Division. Visited 59th Infantry Brigade, 20th Signal Coy, No.32 M.V.S. and noted ophthalmia cases under the new treatment.	

Army Form C. 2118.

WAR DIARY
or
INTELLIGENCE SUMMARY
(Erase heading not required.)

Instructions regarding War Diaries and Intelligence Summaries are contained in F. S. Regs., Part II. and the Staff Manual respectively. Title Pages will be prepared in manuscript.

Place	Date	Hour	Summary of Events and Information	Remarks and references to Appendices
WELSH FARM	26/9/17	—	Visited the 8 Batteries of the 91st & 92nd Bder. R.F.A.	
"	27/9/17	—	Visited No 32 M.V.S. R.A. Hd.Qrts., & examined ophthalmia cases.	
"	28/9/17	—	Visited the R.A. Horse Lines, No 32 M.V.S. and received the A.F. 2000 from the V.Os.	
"	29/9/17	—	Attended Conference & Div. Hd'Qrts. moved to Proven. No 32 M.V.S. moved to	
"	30/9/17	—	seeing Units entrained. Visited No 32 M.V.S.	

T. Lishman
Maj. A.V.C.

D.A.D.V.S.
20TH DIVISION.
No ....
Date ....

WAR DIARY
or
INTELLIGENCE SUMMARY

Army Form C. 2118.

DADVS 20D Vol 17

Place	Date	Hour	Summary of Events and Information	Remarks and references to Appendices
PROVEN	1/10/17		No 32 Mobr. Vety. Sect. entrained for Third Army.	
"	2/10/17		" " " arrived at W.4.C. central sheet 57c.	
"	3/10/17		The whole of the Division left PROVEN for Third Army by train. Divisional Hd Qrs arrived & opened at HAPLINCOURT. (I.34.c.3.5.) sheet 57c	
HAPLINCOURT	3/10/17			
"	4/10/17		Divisional Headquarters moved to PERRONNE.	
PERONNE	5/10/17		Visited the 59th Machine Gun Coy. at Beaucourt & maintained 8 mules & 3 horses about to proceed overseas, & also 10 mules & 1 horse of the 217th M.G.C. at YTRES. Visited No. 3 2 M.V.S. at LE MESNIL & also the D.A.D.V.S., 40th Division at SOREL-LE-GRAND & arranged about the relief on the 9th inst.	
"	6/10/17		Visited the 59th M.G.C. at Hendecourt & 217th M.G.C. at Sorel to inspect animals that had been maintained. All passed the test.	
"	7/10/17		nothing to record.	

Army Form C. 2118.

D.A.D.V.S.
20TH DIVISION

WAR DIARY
or
INTELLIGENCE SUMMARY

(Erase heading not required.)

Instructions regarding War Diaries and Intelligence Summaries are contained in F. S. Regs., Part II. and the Staff Manual respectively. Title Pages will be prepared in manuscript.

Place	Date	Hour	Summary of Events and Information	Remarks and references to Appendices
PERONNE	8/10/17		Nothing to record.	
"	9/10/17		No 32 Mobile Veterinary Section moved to MOISLANS from LE MESNIL.	
"	10/10/17		20th Division Hd.Qtrs. moved from PERONNE to SOREL LE GRAND.	
SOREL-LE-GRAND	11/10/17		No 32 M.V.S. took over site from No 51 M.V.S. at MOISLANS. Looked for a suitable billet for the Advanced Post of M.V.S in FINS. Established Advanced Collecting Post at NURLU.	
"	12/10/17		Visited 61st D.A.C., 61st Dvl.Tpty. Bde. Transport Lines, secured a site at FINS for an Advanced Veterinary Post. Made out & forwarded to A.D.V.S., IIIrd Corps the consolidated A.F.A. 2000 for the week ending 11.10.17.	
"	13/10/17		Attended Conference at office of A.D.V.S. 3rd Corps at CATELET. Visited 40th Div. Amm.Col. & D.A.A. Sect. 20th D.A.C.	
"	14/10/17		Visited 239 Coy (A.T.) R.E., No 3 Sect. 20th D.A.C., 159, 160, & 161 Coys. A.S.C., 20th Signal Coy, Advanced Collecting Post Fins, & No 32 M.V.S. at Moislans. Capt. V.B.WELHAM, A.V.C. proceeded on leave.	
"	15/10/17		M.V.S. & Advanced Section visited, also 62nd Field Ambulance	

2449 Wt. W14957/M90 750,000 1/16 J.B.C. & A. Forms/C.2118/12.

Army Form C. 2118.

WAR DIARY
or
INTELLIGENCE SUMMARY.
(Erase heading not required.)

D.A.D.V.S.
22.4 27633A.

Instructions regarding War Diaries and Intelligence Summaries are contained in F. S. Regs., Part II. and the Staff Manual respectively. Title pages will be prepared in manuscript.

Place	Date	Hour	Summary of Events and Information	Remarks and references to Appendices
SOREL-LE-GRAND	16/10/17	—	Visited 59th Infty. Bde. & M.G.C., and A.D.V.S. IIIrd Corps. inspected No 32 M.V.S. & Advanced Collecting Post.	
"	17/10/17	—	Visited 727 Labour Coy., 108th Labour Coy., 3rd Corps Cyclists Batt. Forwarded completed AFA2000 to A.D.V.S. IIIrd Corps. Visited 59th Infty. Bde.	
"	18/10/17	—	Visited M.V.S. & Advanced Post & 62nd Field Ambulance 59th Infantry Bde.	
"	19/10/17	—	Visited 59th Infantry Bde. & M.G.C. & M.V.S.	
"	20/10/17	—	" M.V.S., 159, 160, & 167 Bde A.D.L. & D.A.A. dochin 20th D.A.L.	
"	21/10/17	—	Visited 59th Infantry Bde. & M.G.C. Advanced Collecting Post. 62nd Field Ambulance & No 32 M.V.S. 20th Division Artillery arrived & received wire from	
"	22/10/17	—	A.D.V.S. XIV th Corps that a case of Horse's contagious had been left in the Corps area by A & B 91 Bde R.F.A.	

Army Form C. 2118.

D.A.D.V.S.,
20TH DIVISION.

No. ....
Date ....

WAR DIARY
or
INTELLIGENCE SUMMARY.
(Erase heading not required.)

Instructions regarding War Diaries and Intelligence Summaries are contained in F. S. Regs., Part II. and the Staff Manual respectively. Title pages will be prepared in manuscript.

Place	Date	Hour	Summary of Events and Information	Remarks and references to Appendices
SORELLE-GRAND	23/10/17	—	Visited 20th Division Artillery & Motr. Vety. Sect.	
"	24/10/17	—	Visited units. Motr. Vety. Sect., & Advanced Collecting Post with A.D.V.S. VIIth Corps	
"	25/10/17	—	D.D.V.S. Third Army, inspected the horses of the 20th Division R.A.	
"	26/10/17	—	Visited 59th Lt. Bde, 159, 160 & 161 Bty A.F.A. & Motr. Vety. Sect. Forwarded consolidated A.F.A. 2000.	
"	27/10/17 28/10/17	—	Attended a Conference with A.D.V.S. VIIth Corps. Visited 'A' Batty 91st Bde R.F.A. to see a suspicious case of stomatitis & 'B' Batty 181 Bde R.F.A. 40 Sim to see suspected case of glanders. Stomatitis case isolated for observation & the Batty put on to separate trough for water. Applied the mallein test to the mule suspected of glanders in 181 Bde R.F.A.	
"	29/10/17	—	The animal tested with mallein on the previous day gave no reaction, the stomatitis case showed nothing typical or definite.	

(A7883) D. D. & L., London, E.C.
Wt. W809/M1672 350,000 4/17 Sch. 52a. Forms/C/2118/14

Army Form C. 2118.

WAR DIARY
or
INTELLIGENCE SUMMARY.
(Erase heading not required.)

D.A.D.V.S.
29th OCT 30th.

Place	Date	Hour	Summary of Events and Information	Remarks and references to Appendices
SOREL-LE-GRAND	30/10/17	—	Took over the duties of A.D.V.S., IIIrd Corps during the temporary absence of Lt. Col. McGowan, A.V.C. while acting for D.D.V.S., IInd Army.	
"	31/10/17		Routine work of Corps in the morning. A Division in the afternoon.	

T. Lishman
Maj. A.V.C.
D.A.D.V.S., 20th Div.

31.10.17

WAR DIARY or INTELLIGENCE SUMMARY

Army Form C. 2118.

D.A.D.V.S.
20TH DIVISION.

Vol 18

Place	Date	Hour	Summary of Events and Information	Remarks and references to Appendices
SOREL-LE-GRAND	1/7		Went to III rd Corps and visited M.V.S. and Divisional work.	
"	2 "		Corps routine; received & forwarded the A.F. A 2000. Visited 59th Infantry Bde.	
"	3 "		Corps routine; Visited M.V.S. & 60th Infantry Bde.	
"	4 "		" Visited 91st Bde R.F.A.	
"	5 "		" Visited M.V.S. & 'A' Batt. 91st Bde R.F.A.	
"	6 "		" & 61st Infantry Bde.	
"	7 "		Issued a typed copy of the G.R.O. laying down the Forage ration to each officer & unit in the Division & had a Divisional Order published drawing each of these Officers to keep a forage account & report any shortage.	
"	8 "		Corps routine; Inspected the animals of 181st Bde R.F.A, 40th Division in consequence of an application for an increased ration.	
"	9 "		Inspect remounts of 2nd/1st Lancs H.A.; Corps routine.	

Army Form C. 2118.

WAR DIARY
or
INTELLIGENCE SUMMARY.
(Erase heading not required.)

D.A.D.V.S.
20TH DIVISION.

Place	Date	Hour	Summary of Events and Information	Remarks and references to Appendices
SOREL-LE-GRAND	10/4/17		Corps routine.	
"	11/4/17		Visited 60th Field Ambulance; Corps Routine.	
"	12/4/17		Corps routine. Inspected animal of 2nd/1st Lances H.A. Bde maze. Evacuated one case.	
"	13/4/17		Corps routine; visited 464 Batty A.F.A. Brown where a case of glanders had been evacuated to Base. Made arrangements for malleining.	
"	14/4/17 15/4/17		Corps routine; 69th in R.A. came under my administration. Corps routine. Visited 464 Batty A.F.A. to see result of malleïn test – all negative. 12th Div Artillery came under my administration.	
"	16/4/17		Corps routine; 29th Divison Artillery came under my administration. Inspected A.F.A. 2000. Handed over to A.D.V.S. IIIrd Corps.	
"	17/4/17		Advanced Vety. Collecting post moved from FINS to SOREL	
"	18/4/17		Attended a conference at office of A.D.V.S. IIIrd Corps to arrange the establishment of a Vety E.G.S.	

Army Form C. 2118.

D.A.D.V.S.,
20TH DIVISION.

No. ....
Date ....

WAR DIARY
or
INTELLIGENCE SUMMARY.
(Erase heading not required.)

Instructions regarding War Diaries and Intelligence Summaries are contained in F. S. Regs., Part II. and the Staff Manual respectively. Title pages will be prepared in manuscript.

Place	Date	Hour	Summary of Events and Information	Remarks and references to Appendices
SOREL-LE-GRAND	19/7	—	Visited the 91st & 92nd Bde. R.F.A. & 60th Infty. Bde.	
"	20/7	—		
"	21/7	—		
"	22/7	—		
"	23/7	—		
"	24/7	—	Inspections made of the whole of the Animals of Transport of the Division	
"	25/7	—		
"	26/7	—		
"	27/7	—		
"	28/7	—		
"	29/7	—	Office moved to Moislains. 10.32 M.V.S. moved to Moislains.	
MOISLAINS	30/7	—	Office moved back to SOREL-LE-GRAND. Adv. Vet. Sect. established at SOREL-LE-GRAND.	

W. Denington Capt. A.V.C.
acting D.A.D.V.S.

Army Form C. 2118.

D.A.D.V.S.
20TH DIVISION.
No. ....
Date ....

WAR DIARY
or
INTELLIGENCE SUMMARY.
(Erase heading not required.)

Instructions regarding War Diaries and Intelligence Summaries are contained in F. S. Regs., Part II. and the Staff Manual respectively. Title pages will be prepared in manuscript.

Place	Date	Hour	Summary of Events and Information	Remarks and references to Appendices
SORELLE	1/12/17	—	Arranging with D.A.D.V.S. 61st Div. to take over	
"	2/12/17	—	Major LISHMAN, D.A.D.V.S. received riding accident by a fall from his horse when inspecting transport. evac. by 61st M.V.S.	
"	3/12/17	—	Capt. W. DENINGTON assumed duties of D.A.D.V.S. vice Major LISHMAN to 3rd Corps rest hospital	
"	4/12/17	—	Moved to BAIZIEUX	
BAIZIEUX	5/12/17	—	9.32 M.V.S. moved by road to MEAULTE	
"	6/12/17	—	Inspected Divisional transport at MEAULTE from Contway moved to HUCQUELIERS.	
HUCQUELIERS	7/12/17	—	Waiting to report	
"	8/12/17	—	Visited A.D.V.S. 10th Corps. 9.32 M.V.S. arrived at WAILLY. M.G. Corps. Mtd G.H. Transport Lines of 59, 60 & 61 Inf. Bde groups	
"	9/12/17	—	Visited Div. Hqrs, Horse Lines and Div. Signals horse lines	
"	10/12/17	—	Visited A.D.V.S. 10th Corps, 59, 60 & 61 Inf Bde groups and 32 M.V.S.	
"	11/12/17	—	Visited Div. Hdqrs and Div Signals Horse Lines. Visited farm of Mr. Charles Dumoulin of Alette for A.P.M. and examined mare with respect to a claim of injury by British motor car	

D. D. & L., London, E.C.
(A7883) Wt. W80g/M1672 550,000 4/17 Sch. 52a. Forms/C/2118/14

Army Form C. 2118.

WAR DIARY
or
INTELLIGENCE SUMMARY.
(Erase heading not required.)

D.A.D.V.S.
20TH DIVISION.
No. ....
Date ....

Instructions regarding War Diaries and Intelligence Summaries are contained in F. S. Regs., Part II. and the Staff Manual respectively. Title pages will be prepared in manuscript.

Place	Date	Hour	Summary of Events and Information	Remarks and references to Appendices
Niepeglin	12/12/17	—	Office moved to BLARINGHEM. M.V.S. moved from WALLY to RACQUINGHEM.	
BLARINGHEM	13/12/17	—	Visit Div Hdqrs Animals, M.V.S., inspected 61st Hy Rle transport passing through. CAPT. E.J.B. SEWELL reported arrival for duty. MAJOR T. LISHMAN, returned from No 41 Stationary Hospital to light duty.	
"	14/12/17	—	Routine work in office. Received weekly returns, made out consolidated A.F.A 2000 forwarded to A.D.V.S., IXth Corps.	
"	15/12/17	—	Routine work in office.	
"	16/12/17	"	" " " "	
"	17/12/17	"	" " " " & visited No 32 M.V.S. & visited all H.2. animals & 2.0th Signals	
"	18/12/17	—	Routine work	
"	19/12/17	"	" "	
"	20/12/17	"	" "	
"	21/12/17	—	Received returns & forwarded consolidated A.F.A 2000 to A.D.V.S., IXth Corps.	

Army Form C. 2118.

WAR DIARY
or
INTELLIGENCE SUMMARY.
(Erase heading not required.)

D.A.D.V.S.,
20TH DIVISION.

Place	Date	Hour	Summary of Events and Information	Remarks and references to Appendices
BLARINGHEM	22/12	—	Visited the animals of the 61st Infy Bde Groups.	
"	23/12	—	Visited No 32 M.V.S.	
"	24/12	—	Routine work in office	
"	25/12	—	Nothing to record.	
"	26/12	—	Proceeded on leave. Capt L W Derrington acting.	
"	27/12	—	Visited Div. Hqrs & Squad C. Horses	
"	28/12	—	Visited 61st Infy Bde Groups.	
"	29/12	—	Visited 60th Infy Bde Group, Div Hqrs & Squad C. Horses	
"	30/12	—	Visited 61st Infy Bde Group and M.V.S.	
"	31/12	—	Accompanied A.D.V.S. on his inspection of 61st Infy Bde.	

W. Derrington Capt AVC
Acting D.A.D.V.S.

Army Form C. 2118.

WAR DIARY
or
INTELLIGENCE SUMMARY.
(Erase heading not required.)

D.A.D.V.S. Vol 20

Instructions regarding War Diaries and Intelligence Summaries are contained in F. S. Regs., Part II, and the Staff Manual respectively. Title pages will be prepared in manuscript.

Place	Date	Hour	Summary of Events and Information	Remarks and references to Appendices
BLARINGHEM	1/1/18	—	Visited 60th Inf. Bde. & amp; 9 pty of 61st Inf. Bde. & groups.	
"	2/1/18	—	Accompanied G.O.C. Div. on his Inspection of 60th Inf. Bde.	
"	3/1/18	—	Visited Div. Hqrs & Signals Horses	
"	4/1/18	—	Accompanied G.O.C. on his Inspection of 59th Bde. M.V.S. and to Conqueror Camp Shelters. M.G.d.S.O.	
"	5/1/18	—	Visited WALLON-CAPPEL & MORBEQUE & see Animals left and arrange dispersal of same.	
"	6/1/18	—	Visited Div Hqrs, Signals & Div Train Horses	
"	7/1/18	—	Office moved to WESTOUTRE. Sheet 28. M.9.C.4.0.	
WESTOUTRE	8/1/18	—	Visited M.V.S. and arranged establishment of Dismounted Animal Rest Station. Visited M.M.P. & Div. Hqrs. horses.	
"	"	—	Visited R.E. Coy. Signals 61st Inf. Bde & 62nd Field Amb.	
"	9	—	9 D.I.I. Transport Lines	
"	10	—	Visited M.V.S.	
"	11	—	Visited 61st Inf. Bde. Capt Derington ceased to act as D.A.D.V.S. Major Lishman D.A.D.V.S. returned from leave.	

Army Form C. 2118.

WAR DIARY
or
INTELLIGENCE SUMMARY.
(Erase heading not required.)

Instructions regarding War Diaries and Intelligence Summaries are contained in F.S. Regs., Part II. and the Staff Manual respectively. Title pages will be prepared in manuscript.

Place	Date	Hour	Summary of Events and Information	Remarks and references to Appendices
Wetutu	12/7/18	—	Attended conference with A.D.V.S. IX th Corps and took completed returns.	
"	13/7/18	—	Visited the Div. H.Q. horses, R.A. Hd Qtrs, R.E. Hd Qtrs, 20th Signal Coy, 61st F.S. Bay A.V.C. Visited No 32 M.V.S. & 61st Field Ambulance proceeded on leave to England.	
"	14/7/18	—	Inspected 158 Coy A.S.C. at dt Jans Battel. Office work	
"	15"	—	Inspected 91st Bde. R.F.A.	
"	16"	—	" 92nd " "	
"	17"	—	" 20th Div. Amm. Col.	
"	18"	—	" 61st Infty Bde, 159, 160 & 161 Coys A.S.C., 217th M.G.C.	
"	19"	—	Took consolidated A.F.A. 2000 to IX Corps for conference with A.D.V.S. & inspected 60th Field Ambulance at Bailleul.	
"	20"	—	Inspected all units of 59th Infty Bde.	
"	21"	—	Took over duties of A.D.V.S., IX th Corps during temporary absence of Col. Bartlett.	
"	22"	—	Routine work at IX th Corps & in the Office	
"	23"	—	" "	

Army Form C. 2118.

WAR DIARY
or
INTELLIGENCE SUMMARY.
(Erase heading not required.)

Place	Date	Hour	Summary of Events and Information	Remarks and references to Appendices
WESTOUTRE	24/1/18	—	Routine work at Corps in Office, Westoutre N° 32 M.V.S.	
"	25"	—	" " "	
"	26"	—	" " "	
"	27"	—	" " "	
"	28"	—	Capt. F.S. Clay returned from leave.	
"	29"	—	Capt. W. Dennington, A.V.C., went on 14 days leave to England.	
"	30"	—	Returned from IX th Corps when it functions were taken over by XXII nd Corps. Inspected 62 nd Field Ambulance and 60 th Infty. Bde.	
"	31"	—	Office work & M.V.S. Arranged about the formation of a rest station for horses at the M.V.S.	

31-1-18

T. Lichman
Maj. A.V.C.
D.A.D.V.S., 20th Division

Army Form C. 2118.

WAR DIARY
or
INTELLIGENCE SUMMARY.
(Erase heading not required.)

ADVS 22nd Division

Vol 21

Place	Date	Hour	Summary of Events and Information	Remarks and references to Appendices
WESTOUTRE	1/2/18	—	Inspected in conjunction with the O.C. 20th Div. Train, the transport of the 61st Infty. Bde. & 61st M.G.C.	
"	2/2/18	—	" " " 59th Infty. Bde. & 59th "	
"	3/2/18	—	Inspected animals of Divisional Headquarters, R.A. Headquarters, R.E., HQ 2nd Bn. M.M.P., & 20th Signal Coy.	
"	4/2/18	—	Inspected with G.C. 20th Div. Train, the 60th Infty. Bde & 60th M.G.C.	
"	5/2/18	—	" " " 20th Div. Amm. Col. Act-M.O. Vety. Section.	
"	6/2/18	—	" " " 20th Divisional Train. Act M.O. Vety. Sect.	
"	7/2/18	—	Inspected the 10th & 11th R.B. in connexion with prevalence of mange.	
"	8/2/18	—	" " " the 83, 84, & 96th Field Coys. R.E. & 11th Batt. D.L.I.	
"	9/2/18	—	Took AFA 2000 to ADVS, XXIInd Corps at ABEELE.	
"	10/2/18	—	Inspected the 10th & 11th R.B. in connexion with outbreak of mange.	
"	11/2/18	—	" " C & D Batteries 92nd Bde R.F.A. Visited M.V.S.	
"	12/2/18	—	Inspected with the O.C. Train the 83rd, 84th, & 96th Field Coys R.E. and 2nd Batt. Scottish Rifles.	
"	13/2/18	—	Inspected A & B Batteries, 92nd Bde R.F.A. Visited M.V.S.	

Army Form C. 2118.

WAR DIARY
or
INTELLIGENCE SUMMARY.
(Erase heading not required.)

D.A.D.V.S.
20th DIVISION

Place	Date	Hour	Summary of Events and Information	Remarks and references to Appendices
WESTOUTRE	14/2/18	—	Received A.F.A 2000 from V.Os & inspected the arrival of the 60th Field Ambulance at Bailleul with the Train.	
"	15/2/18	—	Capt J.B. Welham O.C. No 32 M.V.S. went to Paris on leave for 48 hours. Capt G. Simson A.V.C. proceeded to England on 14 days leave. Visited No 32 M.V.S. & B & C Batty. R.F.A.	
"	16/2/18	—	Took the consolidated return to A.D.V.S. XIInd Corps & attended his conference. No 32 M.V.S. moved to STRAZEELE area.	
"	17/2/18	—	My Office with Div Hd'Qrts moved to BLARINGHEM and No 32 M.V.S. to RACQUINGHEM.	
"	18/2/18	—	Inspected 83rd, 84th & 96th Field bays R.E. & 11th Batt. 9 L.I.	
"	19/2/18	—	" 59th Divl Bde Transport with G.O.C. Division.	
"	20/2/18	—	" 60th & 61st Infantry Bdes.	
"	21/2/18	—	Received A.F.A 2000 from V.O's	
"	22/2/18	—	Division H.Q. & No 32 M.V.S. moved from BLARINGHEM to ERCHEU in Fifth Army Area.	

Army Form C. 2118.

WAR DIARY
INTELLIGENCE SUMMARY.
(Erase heading not required.)

Place	Date	Hour	Summary of Events and Information	Remarks and references to Appendices
ERCHEU	23/2/18	—	Completed the move to ERCHEU. No 32 M.V.S. in same village. Notified arrival to A.D.V.S. XVIII th Corps.	
"	24/2/18	—	Inspected all Hd Qtrs units & received a visit from A.D.V.S. who looked at M.V.S. billet.	
"	25/2/18	—	Inspected 12th Batt. K.R.R.C. Visited M.V.S., arranged changes	
"	26/2/18	—	" 6th K.S.L.I., 7th Oxon Bucks L.I., & 12th R.B., also 60th Field Ambulance	
"	27/2/18	—	Inspected 92nd Bde & 12th Batt. R.B. with A.D.V.S.	
"	28/2/18	—	Inspected 11th K.R.R., 10th R.B., 2nd Scottish Rifles, 159 Coy. A.S.C.	

T. Lishman,
Maj. A.V.C.

D.A.D.V.S.
20TH DIVISION.
No.
Date 28.2.18

WAR DIARY or INTELLIGENCE SUMMARY

Army Form C. 2118.

D.A.D.V.S.
20TH DIVISION.

Place	Date	Hour	Summary of Events and Information	Remarks and references to Appendices
ERCHEU	1/3/18	—	Inspected the 92nd Bde. R.F.A. & despatched the consolidated A.F.A. 2000 to A.D.V.S., XVIIIth Corps.	
"	2/3/18	—	Inspected 20th Div. H.Q., R.E.H.Q., M.M.P., 20th Signal Coy. R.E., No. 32 M.V.S. & routine work in Office	
"	3/3/18	—	Inspected 59th, 60th, 61st & 217th Machine Gun Companies	
"	4/3/18	—	" " 11th Rifle Bde.	
"	5/3/18	—	Office routine & worked = M. de Vatz. hosp. in connexion with the treatment of ophthalmia	
"	6/3/18	—	Inspected 20th Div. Amm. Col.	
"	7/3/18	—	Routine work in Office & receiving A.F.A. 2000	
"	8/3/18	—	Despatched consolidated A.F.A. 2000 to A.D.V.S. XVIIIth Corps.	
"	9/3/18	—	Inspected 7th Somerset L.I.	
"	10/3/18	—	Capt. T.F. ADDISON, A.V.C. (T.C.) reported arrival for duty in the Division vice Capt. W. DENINGTON, A.V.C. (T.C.), to ENGLAND. Inspected 161 Coy. A.S.C.	
"	11/3/18	—	Captain W. DENINGTON, reported departure for England for	

WAR DIARY
or
INTELLIGENCE SUMMARY.
(Erase heading not required.)

Army Form C. 2118.

D.A.D.V.S.,
20TH DIVISION.

Place	Date	Hour	Summary of Events and Information	Remarks and references to Appendices
ERCHEU	12/3/18	—	duty in the Abbeubst Command. Inspected 91st Bde. R.F.A.	
"	13/3/18	—	Inspected 83rd Field Coy. R.E.	
"	13/3/18	—	Inspected with O.C. Div. Train, 20th A.g. Coy. R.E., 60th, 61st, & 62nd Field Ambulances.	
"	14/3/18	—	With A.D.V.S., XVIIIth Corps inspected the 20th Divisional Machine Gun Battalion.	
"	15/3/18	—	Visited 7th Somerset L.I., 2nd Scottish Rifles, & 'A' Batty 92nd Bde. R.F.A. Consolidated A.F. A 2000 sent to A.D.V.S., XVIIIth Corps.	
"	16/3/18	—	Visited 84th Field Coy. R.E. & 12th K.R.R.C.	
"	17/3/18	—	Routine work in office.	
"	18/3/18	—	Visited 11th Batt. D.L.I.	
"	19/3/18	—	" 96th Field Coy. R.E. and 60th Field Ambulance.	
"	20/3/18	—	" 159 Coy, A.S.C., 11th R.B., & 10th R.B.	
"	21/3/18	—	The 20th Divn HdQrs. moved to HAM, M.V.S. moved to Nt SULPICE.	
HAM	22/3/18	—	Removed to ESMERY HALLON, Motr Vehy dept moved to OFFOY	

Army Form C. 2118.

WAR DIARY
or
INTELLIGENCE SUMMARY.
(Erase heading not required.)

Instructions regarding War Diaries and Intelligence Summaries are contained in F. S. Regs., Part II. and the Staff Manual respectively. Title pages will be prepared in manuscript.

Place	Date	Hour	Summary of Events and Information	Remarks and references to Appendices
ESMERY HALLON	23/3/18	—	M.V.S. moved back to ERCHEU during the previous night. My Office & Div. Headquarters moved to NESLE. M.V.S. moved to CARREPUITS.	
NESLE	24/3/18	—	Div. Headquarters & D.A.D.V.S. moved to CARREPUITS	
CARREPUITS	25/3/18	—	Div. rear Hd'Qrts. moved to QUESNEL, M.V.S. moved to HANGEST-EN-SANTERRE.	
HANGEST	26/3/18	—	moved my Office with Mob. Vet. Sect. to CASTEL.	
CASTEL	27/3/18	—	moved Office & M.V.S. to MOREUIL	
MOREUIL	28/3/18	—	moved " " " DOMART-SUR-LA-LUCE.	
DOMART	29/3/18	—	" " " BOVES	
BOVES	30/3/18	—	remained in BOVES	
BOVES	31/3/18	—	moved to SAINS-EN-AMIENOIS, evacuated sick animals to PICQUIGNY.	

T. Lithman
Mj. A.V.C.

D.A.D.V.S.:
20TH DIVISION.
No.
Date.

Army Form C. 2118.

D.A.D.V.S.,
20TH DIVISION.

№ ....
Date ....

WAR DIARY
or
INTELLIGENCE SUMMARY.
(Erase heading not required.)

Instructions regarding War Diaries and Intelligence Summaries are contained in F. S. Regs., Part II. and the Staff Manual respectively. Title pages will be prepared in manuscript.

Place	Date	Hour	Summary of Events and Information	Remarks and references to Appendices
SAINS-EN- AMIENOIS	1/4/18	—	My Office with M.V.S. remaining at SAINS. Sick animals evacuated to PICQVIGNY.	
"	2/4/18	—	M.V.S. remains at SAINS. D.A.D.V.S. in touch with 20th Div. R.A.	
"	3/4/18	—	Office of D.A.D.V.S. moved to 20th Div. H.Q. at NAMPS-AU-MONT Div Hdqtrs & Office of D.A.D.V.S. moved to QUEVAUVILLERS	
QUEVAUVILLERS	4/4/18	—	Packed up to move, but the order was cancelled late in the day.	
"	5/4/18	—	Visited the 20th Machine Gun Batt. at NAMPS-AU-MONT. Received the A.F.A 2000 & forwarded the consolidated return to A.D.V.S., XVIII th Corps.	
"	6/4/18	—	Saw 60 Infty. Bde. Transport on road. Visited CAVILLON arranged with D.A.D.V.S., 8th Division re. evacuation. M.V.S. moved to DURY. Supply Transport & Div. train returned to Div.	
"	7/4/18	—	Routine work in office. Capt T.F.ADDISON, A.V.C. reported his return with Sup Train.	
"	8/4/18	—	Visited Col. Steel, A.D.V.S, 19th Corps at POIX Collecting Area to arrange evacuations.	

Army Form C. 2118.

D.A.D.V.S.
20TH DIVISION.

No. ....
Date ....

WAR DIARY
or
INTELLIGENCE SUMMARY.
(Erase heading not required.)

Instructions regarding War Diaries and Intelligence Summaries are contained in F. S. Regs., Part II. and the Staff Manual respectively. Title pages will be prepared in manuscript.

Place	Date	Hour	Summary of Events and Information	Remarks and references to Appendices
QUEVAUVILLERS	9/4/18	—	Visited R.E. Field Coy at ST AUBIN & No 32 M.V.S. on it arrived at LINCHEUX.	
"	10/4/18	—	Div Hd Qtrs, my office, & No 32 M.V.S. moved to HUPPY	
HUPPY	11/4/18	—	" " moved to GAMACHES	
GAMACHES	12/4/18	—	visited 60th Bde. Hd Qrs., 6th K.S.L.I., 12th K.R.R.C., 159 Coy. A.S.C., 96th Fd. Coy. R.E., & 60th Field Ambulance.	
"	13/4/18	—	Mob. Vet. Sect. moved to BAZINVAL, sent consolidated return to A.D.V.S., XVIII th Corps.	
"	14/4/18	—	Mob. Vety. Section moved to BUIGNY-LES-GAMACHES to be near Abbeville for evacuating sick.	
"	15/4/18	—	Routine work in office & visited M.V.S.	
"	16/4/18	—	The Div standing ready to move.	
"	17/4/18	—	M.V.S. moved to PONT REMY with Divisional Transport.	
"	18/4/18	—	Div Headquarters moved by lorry to VILLERS CHATEL & MINGOVAL in First ARMY area. Transport marching north. Received AE2 A2000	
MINGOVAL	19/4/18	—	Transport still on march north.	

Army Form C. 2118.

D.A.D.V.S.
20TH DIVISION.
No. ....
Date ....

WAR DIARY
or
INTELLIGENCE SUMMARY.
(Erase heading not required.)

Instructions regarding War Diaries and Intelligence Summaries are contained in F. S. Regs., Part II. and the Staff Manual respectively. Title pages will be prepared in manuscript.

Place	Date	Hour	Summary of Events and Information	Remarks and references to Appendices
MINGOVAL	20/4/18	—	Made out consolidated A.F.A 2000, & sent to A.D.V.S. XVIIIth Corps.;	
"	21/4/18	—	M.V.S. arrived in MINGOVAL. Transport of Division arrived.	
"	22/4/18	—	Inspect the nuclei of No 3 Sect, 20th Div. Ammn. Col. Routine in Office. Inspected 20th Machine Gun Batt., 12th K.R.R., 12th R.B., 6th K.S.L.I., 60th Bde. H.Q.; 61st Field Ambulance, 83rd Fld. Coy. R.E., & 160 Coy. A.S.C.	
"	23/4/18	—	Inspected 11th D.L.I., 60th Field Ambulance, 59th Infty. Bde. H.Q., & 2nd Scottish Rifles.	
"	24/4/18	—	Inspected 7th Somerset L.I., 7th D.C.L.I., 84th Fld. Coy. R.E., 11th R.B., 11th K.R.R., 62nd Field Ambulance, 159 & 161 Coys. A.S.C.	
"	25/4/18	—	Inspected with bde., Train, 59th Infantry Bde.	
"	26/4/18	—	" " " 61st Field Ambulance & 60th Infty. Bde.	
"	27/4/18	—	A.F.A 2000 sent to A.D.V.S., XVIIIth Corps.	
"	28/4/18	—	Inspected with 62 Train, 62nd Field Ambulance & 61st Infty. Bde.	
"	29/4/18	—	Inspected 96th Field Coy. R.E.	
"	30/4/18	—	" " 20th Batt. M.G.C. & 11th D.L.I., 61st Field Ambulance.	

T. Lishman
30.4.18   Mj. A.V.C.

WAR DIARY
or
INTELLIGENCE SUMMARY.
(Erase heading not required.)

Army Form C. 2118.

D.A.D.V.S.,
20TH DIVISION.

Place	Date	Hour	Summary of Events and Information	Remarks and references to Appendices
MINGOVAL	1/5/18	—	Visited 83rd Field Coy. R.E. & 60th Field Ambulance.	
"	2/5/18	—	Moved my Office & No 32 M.V.S. with Div. Hd Qrs. to VILLERS-AU-BOIS.V	
VILLERS-AU-BOIS	3/5/18	—	Received weekly returns from V.O.s & consolidated them for A.D.V.S., XVIII th Corps. Visited M.V.S.	
"	4/5/18	—	Looked for new site for M.V.S., Routine work in Office	
"	5/5/18	—	M.V.S. moved to PT SERVINS. Q.29.c.4.1. sheet 36B.	
"	6/5/18	—	Visited 92nd Bde. R.F.A. at GOUY-SERVINS. & M.V.S. at PT SERVINS	
"	7/5/18	—	My Office moved with Div. Hd Qrts to CHATEAU DE LA HAIE W.12.C.7.9. sheet 36B.	
CHATEAU-DE-LA-HAIE	8/5/18	—	Visited 91st Bde. R.F.A., 158 Coy. A.S.C., & Mob. Vety. Sect.	
"	9/5/18	—	" 92nd " " "	
"	10/5/18	—	Consolidating weekly returns a office work. Visited M.V.S.	
"	11/5/18	—	Took A.F.A 2000 to A.D.V.S. Conference at XVIIIth Corps H.Q.	
"	12/5/18	—	Attended a shewing test of cold-shoers. Visited M.V.S. in morning & shoeing board in the afternoon.	

Army Form C. 2118.

WAR DIARY
or
INTELLIGENCE SUMMARY.
(Erase heading not required.)

D.A.D.V.S.
20TH DIVISION

Place	Date	Hour	Summary of Events and Information	Remarks and references to Appendices
CHATEAU-DE-LA-HAIE.	13/5/18	—	Capt P.T. LINDSAY, A.V.C., (S.R.) reported his arrival from command of No 32 M.V.S.	
"	14/5/18	—	Visited A.D.V.S., XVIIIth Corps & 60th Field Ambulance.	
"	15/5/18	—	Visited 61st Infantry Bde, & 159 Coy. A.S.C. & M.V.S.	
"	16/5/18	—	Visited 92nd Bde. R.F.A, 11th D.L.I., 161 Coy. A.S.C., & Mot.Vety.Sect.	
"	17/5/18	—	Visited 59th & 60th Infantry Brigades & M.V.S. Consolidated weekly A.F.A. 2000; Capt J.B. Welham, A.V.C. left for 13th V.E.S. after handing over No 32 M.V.S. to Capt P.T. Lindsay, A.V.C. (S.R.) Visited M.V.S.	
"	18/5/18	—	Visited 60th Infantry Bde & 160 Coy A.S.C.	
"	19/5/18	—	Visited 83rd Field Coy. R.E. & M.V.S.	
"	20/5/18	—	Visited 60th Infantry Bde. & M.V.S.	
"	21/5/18	—	Visited 92nd Bde. R.F.A & M.V.S	
"	22/5/18	—	Visited 91st Bde. R.F.A. & 158 Coy. A.S.C.	
"	23/5/18	—	Visited 11th D.L.I, 61st A.62nd Field Ambulances, & Inspected 92nd Bde. R.F.A with A.D.V.S, XVIIIth Corps.	

Army Form C. 2118.

No C 24

WAR DIARY
or
INTELLIGENCE SUMMARY.
(Erase heading not required.)

D.A.D.V.S.
20TH DIVISION

Place	Date	Hour	Summary of Events and Information	Remarks and references to Appendices
Chateau de La Haie	24/5/18	—	Consolidating A.F.A 2000 & Office work, & at M.V.S.	
"	25/5/18	—	Visited 96th Field Coy. R.E. & 59th Infantry Bde.	
"	26/5/18	—	Routine work in office & visited M.V.S	
"	27/5/18	—	Visited 84th Field Coy. R.E. & 60th Infantry Bde.	
"	28/5/18	—	Visited 20th Divn Ammn. Col. & M.V.S	
"	29/5/18	—	D.D.V.S. First Army inspected Mob. Vety. Sect.	
"	30/5/18	—	Visited 59th Infantry Bde.	
"	31/5/18	—	Consolidated the weekly A.F.A 2000 & visited the A.D.V.S., XVIII th Corps.	

T. Lehmann
Maj. A.V.C.
D.A.D.V.S., 20th Divn.

31.5.18

Army Form C. 2118.

WAR DIARY
or
INTELLIGENCE SUMMARY.
(Erase heading not required.)

Instructions regarding War Diaries and Intelligence Summaries are contained in F. S. Regs., Part II. and the Staff Manual respectively. Title pages will be prepared in manuscript.

D.A.D.V.S.
20TH DIVISION.

Place	Date	Hour	Summary of Events and Information	Remarks and references to Appendices
CHATEAU-DE-LA-HAIE	1/8	—	Visited 61st Infantry Bde. & M.V.S.	
"	2/8	—	" No 3 Section 20th D.A.C. & M.V.S.	
"	3/8	—	" 158 Coy. A.S.C.	
"	4/8	—	Inspected Div. H.Q., 20th Sig. Coy., M.M.P., & M.V.S. Visited A.D.V.S., XVIIIth Corps	
"	5/8	—	Visited 83rd Field Coy. R.E., 159 & 161 Coys A.S.C., & M.V.S	
"	6/8	—	" 61st Infantry Bde., 62nd Field Ambulance & 83rd Field Coy. R.E.	
"	7/8	—	Consolidated A.F.A. 2000 & visited M.V.S.	
"	8/8	—	Visited 20th Machine Gun Batt. & M.V.S.	
"	9/8	—	Routine work in Office	
"	10/8	—	Visited 92nd Bde. R.F.A. & inspected 66 Remounts at M.V.S.	
"	11/8	—	Visited 91st Bde. R.F.A. & took over from A.D.V.S. his duties at XVIIIth Corps.	
"	12/8	—	Left 20th Division and took over temporarily from A.D.V.S., XVIIIth Corps.	
"	13/8 to 23/8	—	Routine work daily in Office	
"	24/8	—	A.D.V.S., XVIIIth Corps returned & I returned to 20th Division. Visited 32 M.V.S., 60th & 61st Field Ambulances, 20th Sig. Coy., Div. H.Q.	

Army Form C. 2118.

WAR DIARY
or
INTELLIGENCE SUMMARY.
(Erase heading not required.)

D.A.D.V.S.,
20TH DIVISION.

No ....
Date ....

Instructions regarding War Diaries and Intelligence Summaries are contained in F. S. Regs., Part II. and the Staff Manual respectively. Title pages will be prepared in manuscript.

Place	Date	Hour	Summary of Events and Information	Remarks and references to Appendices
Chateau-de-la Haie	25/6/18	—	Visited 32 M.V.S., and disposing of accumulated office work.	
"	26/6/18	—	Inspected 59th & 60th Infantry Bdes.	
"	27/6/18	—	" 84th & 96th Field Coy. R.E., 160 Coy. A.S.C. & 32 M.V.S.	
"	28/6/18	—	" 91st Bde. R.F.A. & 158 Coy. A.S.C., & No. 3 Section D.A.C.	
"	29/6/18	—	" Nos. 2 & 3 Sections D.A.C. Forwarded returns to A.D.V.S.	
"	30/6/18	—	Routine work & making out monthly reports.	

T. Lishman,
Major, A.V.C.

D.A.D.V.S.
20TH DIVISION.
No ....
Date 30 · 6 · 18

WAR DIARY
or
INTELLIGENCE SUMMARY
(Erase heading not required.)

Army Form C. 2118.

Place	Date	Hour	Summary of Events and Information	Remarks and references to Appendices
CHATEAU-DE-LA-HAIE	1/7/18	—	Inspected 'C' Battery 91st Bde R.F.A. in connexion with a recent case of mange & M.V.S.	
"	2/7/18	—	Inspected animals & lines of 59th Infty Bde.	
"	3/7/18	—	11th Batt. D.L.I., & 91st Bde. R.F.A. & M.V.S.	
"	4/7/18	—	62nd Fld. Ambulance & 20th Batt. M.G.C.	
"	5/7/18	—	Attended office of A.D.V.S. VIIIth Corps. Received returns.	
"	6/7/18	—	Inspected 2nd Scottish Rifles in which a case of mange had occurred. Visited M.V.S.	
"	7/7/18	—	Routine work	
"	8/7/18	—	Proceeded to VIIIth Corps & took over duties of A.D.V.S. from Col. Nicol who was proceeding on leave.	
"	9/7/18 to 22/7/18	—	Routine work	
"	23/7/18	—	Handed over to Lt Col. Nicol & returned to 20th Div.	
"	24/7/18	—	Major T. Lishman, D.A.D.V.S. proceeded on 10 days leave in France	
"	25/7/18	—	& Capt. F. Thursby A.V.C. took over duties of D.A.D.V.S.	

Army Form C. 2118.

WAR DIARY
or
INTELLIGENCE SUMMARY.
(Erase heading not required.)

D.A.D.V.S.
20TH DIVISION.

No. ....
Date ....

Instructions regarding War Diaries and Intelligence Summaries are contained in F. S. Regs., Part II. and the Staff Manual respectively. Title pages will be prepared in manuscript.

Place	Date	Hour	Summary of Events and Information	Remarks and references to Appendices
Chateau-de-la-Haie	26/7/18 to 31/7/18	—	Routine work of D.A.D.V.S. Open and shutting of 32nd Mobile Vety. Section.	
			R.Hinsley, Capt. A.V.C. a/DADVS. 20th Division.	

WAR DIARY
or
INTELLIGENCE SUMMARY.
(Erase heading not required.)

Army Form C. 2118.

D.A.D.V.S.
20th DIVISION.
No. V/24/331.
Date. 31/8/18

Vol 27

Place	Date	Hour	Summary of Events and Information	Remarks and references to Appendices
CHATEAU-DE-LA-HAIE	2/8/18	—	Major Lishman returned from leave.	
"	3/8/18	—	Visited 59th & 60th Infy. Bdes., 2 A.A. section 20th D.A.E. & No. 32 M.V.S.	
"	4/8/18	—	Visited M.V.S. & A.D.V.S., VIIIth Corps.	
"	5/8/18	—	Visited 83rd Fld. Coy. R.E., 159 & 160 Coy. A.S.C., 61st Infy. Bde. M.V.S. & 11th D.L.I. Capt. W. Andrew A.V.C. reported his arrival for duty with the Div. Vice Capt. G. Simmons evacuated to England sick.	
"	6/8/18	—	Inspected 92nd Bde. R.F.A.	
"	7/8/18	—	Visited 84th & 96th Field Coys. R.E., 160 Coy. A.S.C., and 20th M.G. Batt. Visited M.V.S.	
"	8/8/18	—	Inspected 20th Div. Train. Received a consolidated A.E. A2000. Visited M.V.S.	
"	9/8/18	—	Inspected 91st Bde. R.F.A. & 158 Coy. A.S.C.	
"	10/8/18	—	Inspected 20 Div. Amy. Col. Visited M.V.S.	
"	11/8/18	—	Visited A.D.V.S., VIIIth Corps.	

Army Form C. 2118.

WAR DIARY
or
INTELLIGENCE SUMMARY.
(Erase heading not required.)

D.A.D.V.S.,
20TH DIVISION.

No. V.20/331.
Date. 31/8/15.

Instructions regarding War Diaries and Intelligence Summaries are contained in F. S. Regs., Part II. and the Staff Manual respectively. Title pages will be prepared in manuscript.

Place	Date	Hour	Summary of Events and Information	Remarks and references to Appendices
CHATEAU-DE-LAHAIE	12/8	—	Visited 92nd Bde. R.F.A. & M.V.S. & 60th & 62 Fd. Ambulance	
"	13/8	—	Visited 61st Infantry Bde. & 62nd Field Ambulance	
"	14/8	—	" 59th & 60th Infty. Bdes.	
"	15/8	—	Attended A.D.V.S. Conference. Inspected M.V.S.	
"	16/8	—	Visited M.V.S. Preparing A.F. A2000.	
"	17/8	—	Visited 83rd Field Coy. R.E., 159 Coy. A.S.C., 61st Infty. Bde.	
"	18/8	—	Visited A.D.V.S. Corps & Routine work.	
"	19/8	—	" 59th & 60th Infty. Bdes.	
"	20/8	—	Major T. Lithman proceeded on 14 days leave to England. Capt. P.T. Lindsay took over duties of A/DADVS.	
"	21/8/15	—	Routine work of DADVS Office & duties of M.V.S.	
"	22/8/15	—	Prepared A.F. 2000 & attached units. Visited 60th Inf. Bde. work of M.V.S.	
"	23/8/15	—	Prepared A.F. 2000 of 20th Div. Visited 92nd Bde. R.F.A.	
"	24/8/15	—	Routine work of DADVS office & duties of M.V.S.	
"	25/8/15	—	Routine of DADVS office. Duties of M.V.S. Inspected Transport of Div. H.Q.	
"	26/8/15	—	Routine work of DADVS. & duties of M.V.S.	

Army Form C. 2118.

WAR DIARY
or
INTELLIGENCE SUMMARY.
(Erase heading not required.)

D.A.D.V.S.,
20TH DIVISION.
No. V20/331
Date. 31.8.18

Place	Date	Hour	Summary of Events and Information	Remarks and references to Appendices
CHATEAU DE-LA HAIE	27/8/18	—	Routine work of D.A.D.V.S. Officer & Orderlies of M.V.S.	
	28/8/18	—	"	
	29/8/18	—	Prepared A.F. 2008 of attached units & return of M.V.S.	
	30/8/18	—	Prepared A.F. 2008 of 20th Division. Visited 91st & 13th R.F.A. with A.D.V.S.	
	31/8/18	—	Prepared Monthly Returns. Routine of D.V.S.	

A Lindsay Capt AVC

WAR DIARY or INTELLIGENCE SUMMARY

Army Form C.

D.A.D.V.S., 20TH DIVISION.

Vol 28

Place	Date	Hour	Summary of Events and Information	Remarks and references to Appendices
CHATEAU DE LA HAIE	1/9/18	—	Routine work of DADVS, Officer i/c Antries & M.V.S.	
"	2/9/18	—	"	
"	3/9/18	—	Capt. Clay proceeds on 14 days leave to England.	
"	4/9/18	—	Routine work of DADVS, Offrs i/c Antries & M.V.S.	
"	5/9/18	—	Major Liebman returned from leave.	
				By Linekar Capt AVC
"	6/9/18	—	Inspected 160 Coy. A.S.C., 96th Fld. Coy. R.E., & 32 M.V.S.	
"	7/9/18	—	" 92nd Bde. R.F.A.	
"	8/9/18	—	Routine work & visited A.D.V.S., VIII th Corps, & M.V.S.	
"	9/9/18	—	Visited 59th Infantry Bde. & M.V.S.	
"	10/9/18	—	Inspected 83rd Fld. Coy. R.E., 159 & 161 Coys. A.S.C. & 61st Infty. Bde.	
"	11/9/18	—	Inspected 62nd Field Amb., 11th D.L.I., 20th Batt. M.G.C., & 20th Sig. Coy.	
"	12/9/18	—	Visited 59th Infty. Bde., 60th Infty. Bde., No 3 Sect. 20th D.A.C. and M.V.S.	

Army Form C. 2118.

WAR DIARY
or
INTELLIGENCE SUMMARY.
(Erase heading not required.)

D.A.D.V.S.
20TH DIVISION

Place	Date	Hour	Summary of Events and Information	Remarks and references to Appendices
CHATEAU- DE-LA HAIE	13/9/18	—	Inspected No 1 & 2 Sects, 20th D.A.C., & M.V.S.	
"	14/9/18	—	Inspected 158 Boy. A.S.C., & 91st Bde. R.F.A. Visited M.V.S.	
"	15/9/18	—	Routine work & visited A.D.V.S., & M.V.S.	
"	16/9/18	—	Inspected 84th Field Coy. R.E. & LA TARGETTE & visited M.V.S. Inspected 60th & 61st Fld. Ambulances	
"	17/9/18	—	Visited 20th Batt. M.G.C. & 160 Boy. A.S.C. & M.V.S.	
"	18/9/18	—	Inspected 92nd Bde. R.F.A.	
"	19/9/18	—	Received & communicated A.F.a. A 2000	
"	20/9/18	—	Inspected 59th & 60th Infty. Bdes., 96th Field Coy. R.E., & 20th Signal Company.	
"	21/9/18	—	Inspected 91st Bde. R.F.A., & 158 Coy. A.S.C. & M.V.S.	
"	22/9/18	—	Routine work & visited M.V.S. Visited A.D.V.S., 8th Corps.	
"	23/9/18	—	Visited 83rd Fld. Coy. R.E., 159 & 161 Coys. A.S.C., & 61st Infantry Bde.	
"	24/9/18	—	Visited refilling dump, 20th Batt. M.G.C., 11th Batt. D.L.I. and 62nd Field Ambulance.	
"	25/9/18	—	Attended Conference on shipping at Office of A.D.V.S., 8th Corps.	

Army Form C. 2118.

D.A.D.V.S.,
20TH DIVISION.
No.
Date.

WAR DIARY
or
INTELLIGENCE SUMMARY.
(Erase heading not required.)

Instructions regarding War Diaries and Intelligence Summaries are contained in F. S. Regs., Part II. and the Staff Manual respectively. Title pages will be prepared in manuscript.

Place	Date	Hour	Summary of Events and Information	Remarks and references to Appendices
CHATEAU-DE-LA-HAIE.	26/8 9	—	Visited 12th Batt. K.R.R., & D.A.D.V.S., 20th Division regarding Equipment of A.V.S. dept's with Field kinks, published order about clipping of horses heels. Visited M.V.S.	
"	27/8	—	Routine work & visited M.V.S. & M.M.R. stables.	
"	28/8	—	Visited 59th & 60th Infantry Bdes.	
"	29/8	—	Visited A.D.V.S., 8th Corps.	
"	30/8	—	Visited Headquarters stables, M.V.S., & routine work for end of month.	

T. Lishman,
Maj. A.V.C.,
D.A.D.V.S., 20th Division.

Army Form C. 2118.

WAR DIARY
or
INTELLIGENCE SUMMARY.
(Erase heading not required.)

Place	Date	Hour	Summary of Events and Information	Remarks and references to Appendices
CHATEAU-DE-LA-HAIE.	1/10/18	—	Inspected 160 Coy A.S.C., 158 Coy A.S.C., 96th Fd. Coy. R.E., & 20th D.A.C.; Visited M.V.S.	
"	2/10/18	—	Accompanied A.D.V.S., VIII th Corps on an inspection of all the animals & wagon & transport lines of 20th Division.	
"	3/10/18	—	Received returns from V.O. & visited the animals of the 20th Div. R.A. French Mortar Battery at LA TARGETTE.	
"	4/10/18	—	Visited the 59th & 60th Infty. Bdes, & 158 Coy A.S.C.	
"	5/10/18	—	Arranging the Veterinary part of the relief in the line of the 20th Division by the 12th Division.	
"	6/10/18	—	Div. Hd. Qrs. moved to VILLERS CHATEL & VILLERS CHATEL & N°32 M.V.S. to MINGOVAL	
VILLERS CHATEL	7/10/18	—	Visited N°3 Sect. 20th D.A.C., & 60th Field Ambulance. Capt. P.T. Lindsay i/c 32 M.V.S. proceeded on 14 days leave to England.	
"	8/10/18	—	Visited 83rd Fd. Coy. R.E., 11 Batt. 9.L.I. & M.V.S.	
"	9/10/18	—	" M.V.S. 59th Infty. Bde., 159 Coy. A.S.C., & 84th & 96th Fd. Coy. R.E.	
"	10/10/18	—	Visited M.V.S., & prepared weekly returns.	
"	11/10/18	—	Visited 60th & 61st Infty Bdes, 61st & 62nd Ft. Ambulance, 20th Batt. M.G.C., 160 & 161 Coy A.S.C. and M.V.S.	

Army Form C. 2118.

WAR DIARY
or
INTELLIGENCE SUMMARY.
(Erase heading not required.)

Instructions regarding War Diaries and Intelligence Summaries are contained in F. S. Regs., Part II. and the Staff Manual respectively. Title pages will be prepared in manuscript.

Place	Date	Hour	Summary of Events and Information	Remarks and references to Appendices
VILLERS CHATEL	12/10/18	—	Visited M.V.S., A.D.V.S., 8th Corps.	
"	13/10/18	—	Visited M.V.S., 83rd Fld. Coy. R.E., & 11th D.L.I.	
"	14/10/18	—	" 60th Fld. Ambulance, N°3 Sect. 20th D.A.C.	
"	15/10/18	—	" A.D.V.S., 8th Corps.	
"	16/10/18	—	" 59th Infty. Bde., 84th & 96th Fld. Coy. R.E. & M.V.S.	
"	17/10/18	—	" Kinsgliverpool, 161 Bde. A.S.C., 7th Armnt L.I., 62nd Bde H.Q. A.M.V.S.	
"	18/10/18	—	Routine work in Office & at M.V.S.	
"	19/10/18	—	Visited 83rd Fld. Coy. R.E., 11th Batt. D.L.I., M.V.S., A.D.V.S. Corps.	
"	20/10/18	—	Routine work in Office & at M.V.S.	
"	21/10/18	—	Visited 12 K.R.R., 12th R.B. 61 Fld. Ambulance, 160 Bde. A.S.C., 6th K.S.L.I., 20th Batt. M.G.C., 62nd Fld. Ambulance.	
"	22/10/18	—	Visited 11th K.R.R., 84th & 96th Fld. Coys R.E., D.D.V.S., First Army. Inspected M.V.S.	
"	23/10/18	—	Capt. Lindsey, Lt. 32 M.V.S. returned from leave. Visited 11th K.R.R., 11th R.B. & 159 Bde. A.S.C.	
"	24/10/18	—	Visited 83rd Fld. Coy. R.E. & 11th D.L.I.	

Army Form C. 2118.

WAR DIARY
or
INTELLIGENCE SUMMARY.

(Erase heading not required.)

D.A.D.V.S.,
20th DIVISION.

Place	Date	Hour	Summary of Events and Information	Remarks and references to Appendices
VILLERS CHATEL	25/10/18	—	Dept consolidated A.F.A 2000 to A.D.V.S. VIIIth Corps. Visited First Army Field Remount Section at FREVILLERS.	
"	26/10/18	—	Routine work. Visited 11th K.R.R., & M.V.S.,	
"	27/10/18	—	Visited #s 87 & 96 Fd. Coys R.E., & M.V.S.	
"	28/10/18	—	D.D.V.S., First Army inspected the Division.	
"	29/10/18	—	Routine work & at M.V.S.; inspected 8 cases of frost a month divisions at CAMBLAIN L'ABBE	
"	30/10/18	—	Received orders to move to Third Army (17th Corps)	
"	31/10/18	—	Moving.	

T. Lithman,
Maj. A.V.C.,
D.A.D.V.S., 20th Division

Army Form C. 2118.

D.A.D.V.S.,
20TH DIVISION.
No.
Date

WAR DIARY
or
INTELLIGENCE SUMMARY.
(Erase heading not required.)

Instructions regarding War Diaries and Intelligence Summaries are contained in F. S. Regs., Part II. and the Staff Manual respectively. Title pages will be prepared in manuscript.

Vol 31

Place	Date	Hour	Summary of Events and Information	Remarks and references to Appendices
CAMBRAI	1/8	—	Office & No 32 M.V.S. established at CAMBRAI.	
"	2 "	—	Received visit from A.D.V.S., XVII th Corps.	
"	3 "	—	Office moved to AVESNES-LEZ-AUBERT & M.V.S. to RIEUX standing by for orders to move.	
AVESNES	4 "	—	"	
"	5 "	—	"	
"	6 "	—	Office & M.V.S. moved to VENDEGIES	
VENDEGIES	7 "	—	Visited units of the Division & routine work.	
"	8 "	—	Office & M.V.S. moved to WARGNIES-LE-GRAND.	
WARGNIES	9 "	—	" " BAVAY	
BAVAY	10 "	—	Routine work.	
FEIGNIES	11 "	—	Office moved to FEIGNIES & M.V.S. remained at BAVAY STATION	
"	12 "	—	Visited M.V.S. at BAVAY & A.D.V.S. 17th Corps.	
"	13 "	—	Inspecting 91st Bde R.F.A.	
"	14 "	—	"	
"	15 "	—	" 92nd "	
"	16 "	—	Visited R.E. Field Coys.	

Army Form C. 2118.

WAR DIARY
or
INTELLIGENCE SUMMARY.
(Erase heading not required.)

D.A.D.V.S.
20TH DIVISION.
No. .... Date ....

Instructions regarding War Diaries and Intelligence Summaries are contained in F. S. Regs., Part II. and the Staff Manual respectively. Title pages will be prepared in manuscript.

Place	Date	Hour	Summary of Events and Information	Remarks and references to Appendices
FEIGNIES	17/8	—	Nothing to record	
"	18/8	—	Visited M.V.S. & looked round headquarter units.	
"	19/8	—	" 61st Infantry Bde.	
"	20/8	—	Nothing to record.	
"	21/8	—	Inspected all likely areas for breeding in the Division less R.A., 83rd Fld. Coy. R.E. & 60th Field Ambulance	
"	22/8	—	Forwarded weekly return to A.D.V.S., XVIIth Corps.	
"	23/8	—	Division moved to ~~Rieux~~ WARGNIES-LE-GRAND, M.V.S. to JENLAIN	
WARGNIES-LE-GRAND	24/8	—	Nothing to record	
"	25/8	—	M.V.S. moved to VENDEGIES.	
"	26/8	—	Office & M.V.S. moved to RIEUX	
RIEUX	27/8	—	Nothing to record.	
"	28/8	—	Office & M.V.S. moved to CAMBRAI	
CAMBRAI	29/8	—	M.V.S. moved with transport of 20th Division to Beugnatre.	
"	30/8	—	" to P.A.S. Office of A.D.V.S. remaining at CAMBRAI	

T. Lishman Maj. A.V.C.
D.A.D.V.S., 20th Div.

WAR DIARY or INTELLIGENCE SUMMARY.

Army Form C. 2118.

(Erase heading not required.)

Instructions regarding War Diaries and Intelligence Summaries are contained in F. S. Regs., Part II. and the Staff Manual respectively. Title pages will be prepared in manuscript.

D.A.D.V.S.
20TH DIVISION

Place	Date	Hour	Summary of Events and Information	Remarks and references to Appendices
PAS	1/2/18	—	Offices & M.V.S. established at PAS.	
"	2/2/18	—	Billetting in area.	
"	3/2/18	—	Selecting brood mares from 92nd Bde. R.F.A. & D.A.E.	
"	4/2/18	—	" " " " 91st " " & D.A.E.	
"	5/2/18	—	Visited Second & Cuttish Rifles at TOUTENCOURT.	
"	6/2/18	—	" " 3rd Feb. Bay. & 11th D.L.I.	
"	7/2/18	—	Inspected A/91 Batty. I.R.F.A. in connexion with a case of mange.	
"	8/2/18	—	Visited 60th Bde. H.Q., 6th K.S.L.I., 7th D.C.L.I., & 7th Somerset L.I.	
"	9/2/18	—	Engaged with Corps Committee inspecting & branding brood mares.	
"	10/2/18	—	D.A.D.V.S. proceeded on 10 days French leave, Capt. F.S. Clay A.V.C. acting D.A.D.V.S.	
"	11 "	—		
"	12 "	—		
"	13 "	—	Capt F.S. Clay carried on routine work.	
"	14 "	—		
"	15 "	—		
"	16 "	—		

WAR DIARY or INTELLIGENCE SUMMARY

Army Form C. 2118.

D.A.D.V.S. 20th DIVISION

Place	Date	Hour	Summary of Events and Information	Remarks and references to Appendices
PAS	17/12/18	—		
"	18"	—	Capt Blay carried on renovation work.	
"	19"	—		
"	20"	—		
"	21"	—	Maj. LISHMAN returned from leave.	
"	22"	—	Routine work & demobilisation. Visited M.V.S.	
"	23"	—	", & visited G.H.Q. Committee in selection of mares.	
"	24"	—	Visited A.D.V.S. 17th Corps.	
"	25"	—	Nothing to record.	
"	26"	—	Arranging classification of all animals for demobilisation.	
"	27"	—	Proceeded to 17th Corps Hd Qrs, BEAUQUESNES, to act for A.D.V.S., proceeding on leave to England. Capt Blay to act as D.A.D.V.S.	
"	28"	—	Inspected A & B Batts, 91st & 2nd V3all RHA at Gaudiempré, Inspected C.I.D. Boots 91st RGA at HUMBERCAMP.	
"	29"			
"	30"		Inspected & classified for demobilisation the animals of 59th, 60th, 61st Infantry Brde, 66th Field Ambulance, 159 A.S.C.	

Army Form C. 2118.

WAR DIARY
or
INTELLIGENCE SUMMARY.
(Erase heading not required.)

D.A.D.V.S.
20TH DIVISION.

Instructions regarding War Diaries and Intelligence Summaries are contained in F. S. Regs., Part II. and the Staff Manual respectively. Title pages will be prepared in manuscript.

Place	Date	Hour	Summary of Events and Information	Remarks and references to Appendices
PAS.	31/12/16	—	Inspected A9 & B all R.A.A. which Battery served came of many have been relieved. Inspected A92 Batteries. J.S. Blannis Capt. a/DADVS 2 and Division a/DADVS	

WAR DIARY
INTELLIGENCE SUMMARY

Army Form C. 2118.

Place	Date	Hour	Summary of Events and Information	Remarks and references to Appendices
Pau	1.1.19		Classified animals of 61st Amb[ulance] 61st Bn HQ RK my (sup) 161 Co. A.S.C.	
	2.1.19		Classified animals of Commn S.L. D.C.&L.	
	3.1.19		Classified animals of HQ. A & B Bty 91 Bde R.F.A.	
	4.1.19		" " 92nd Bde R.F.A.	
	5.1.19		" " 13th Co A.S.C.	
	6.1.19		" " H.Q. D.A.C. No 1 & 2 Sec D.A.C.	
	7.1.19		" " R.A.W.S. + hence move	
	8.1.19		Visit 91st Bde R.F.A.	
	9.1.19		Classified animals of 166 Co. R.A.S.C. + 12 R.R.C. Capt f.m. remounted R.A.V.S. I.T. arrived & return with 91st Bde R.F.A.	
	10.1.19		Classified animals of No 3 Sec D.A.C. + 11 D.S.S. Cav Andrew Left this Division for Div HQ. with 232 omm ma I.T.A. office routine	
	11.1.19			
	12.1.19		Classified animals of Div HQ.	

Army Form C. 2118.

D.A.D.V.S.
20TH DIVISION.
No ....
Date ....

WAR DIARY
or
INTELLIGENCE SUMMARY.
(Erase heading not required.)

Instructions regarding War Diaries and Intelligence Summaries are contained in F. S. Regs., Part II. and the Staff Manual respectively. Title pages will be prepared in manuscript.

Place	Date	Hour	Summary of Events and Information	Remarks and references to Appendices
Pau	13.1.19		Clipped animals of 12 R.B. & 62 Field Amb.	
	14.1.19		Visit 9 & M.F.C. RAE	
	15.1.19		Selection of Claus & Veterinary cases for sale at Oulem	
	16.1.19		Office Routine	
	17.1.19		Major J. Silmon R.A.V.C. took over duties of Court & S. Clair R.A.V.C. A.D.V.S. Corps	
	18.1.19		Completed Mallein Test of DADVS 20th Div.	
	19.1.19		Applied mallein test to 50 Y. Lines of 91 Bde R.F.A.	
	20.1.19		" " " R.A.V.C. 91 Bde R.F.A.	
	21.1.19		Inspected 50 Y. Lines & F.A. detach A.S.C. Div	
	22.1.19		Office Routine	
	23.1.19		"	
	24.1.19		Applied mallein test to horses of 2 D.M.G. Bn.	
	25.1.19		Visit 9 Navy R.F.A. & No 3 Sec. D.A.C.	
	26.1.19		Inspected 177 Y. Lines & F.A. detach No 13 Amn. Sub Park	
	27.1.19		Visit R.A. 139, 9 & 2nd 13ad R.F.A.	

Army Form C. 2118.

WAR DIARY
or
INTELLIGENCE SUMMARY.
(Erase heading not required.)

Instructions regarding War Diaries and Intelligence Summaries are contained in F. S. Regs., Part II. and the Staff Manual respectively. Title pages will be prepared in manuscript.

D.A,D.V.S.
25th DIVISION.
No. ....
Date ....

Place	Date	Hour	Summary of Events and Information	Remarks and references to Appendices
Par.	28.1.19		Office Routine	
	29.1.19		Inoculated 2 S.T. men before dep. to Rome	
	30.1.19		Inspection M.V.C.	
	31.1.19		Office Routine	
				A. E. Clare Cowie A.V.C. a/D.A.D.V.S. 25 Div.

WAR DIARY
or
INTELLIGENCE SUMMARY.
(Erase heading not required.)

Army Form C. 2118.

D.A.D.V.S.
20TH DIVISION.

Place	Date	Hour	Summary of Events and Information	Remarks and references to Appendices
Pou	1.2.19.		Visit to M.V.S. & Office Routine	
	2/2/19		Inspected A&B Bats. 92 & 93 Bde R.F.A. & Gaudiempré	
	3/2/19		Classified animals of 3rd A.M.R. Corps at Basseux	
	4/2/19		Visit M.V.S. & M3 Sec D.A.C.	
	5/2/19		Inspected A&B Bats 92 & 93 Bde R.F.A.	
	6/2/19		Routine work in Office	
	7/2/19			
	8/2/19		Visit M.V.S.	
	9/2/19		Office Routine	
	10/2/19		Examined 60 Z Horses at MARIEUX. put on lookahatch	
	11/2/19		Inspected 101 Y Horses at MARIEUX. put to detached	
	12/2/19		Visit M3 Sec. D.A.C. & M.V.S.	
	13/2/19		Applied Mallein test to 72 animals of 28 R Inal Co.	
			& 14 animals of M.M.P. at P.A.S.	
	14/15/2/19		Office Routine	
	16/2/19		Inspected 3 D 2 Horses from R.A. & M.G.C. put Yphalach	
			Applied mallein test to all animals of 59 army F Bae	
			15 g C.D.A.C. & 1st Field Ambulance	

Army Form C. 2118.

WAR DIARY
or
INTELLIGENCE SUMMARY.
(Erase heading not required.)

Instructions regarding War Diaries and Intelligence Summaries are contained in F. S. Regs., Part II. and the Staff Manual respectively. Title pages will be prepared in manuscript.

D.A.D.V.S.
20TH DIVISION.

Place	Date	Hour	Summary of Events and Information	Remarks and references to Appendices
Pas.	17/10		Visit in Sec D.A.C. & M.V.S.	
	18/10		Inspected A & B Batts. 92 & 93 Bde R.F.A. & 84 Fed Co.RE.	
	19/10		Inspected 54 Div. lines at MARIEUX. Men on surface	
	20/10		Office Routine	
	21/10		Visit C & D Batts 92 Bde R.F.A. at HUMBERCAMP.	
	22/10		Office Routine	
	23/10		Visit 61 Inf. Bde — in LOUVENCOURT area.	
	24/10		Visit M.V.S. & R.A. HQ.	
	25/10		Visit A & B Batts. 92 & 93 Bdes R.F.A.	
	26/10		Animals fallen next to 35 animals of 20 in M.9.	
	27/10		Inspected 200 2 animals at MARIEUX fins to attacked	
	28/10			

J. S. Clow
Capt. R.A.V.C.
A.D.V.S. 20 Div.

D.A.D.V.S.
20TH DIVISION.
No ....
Dated 8/11/19.

WAR DIARY or INTELLIGENCE SUMMARY

Army Form C. 2118.

D.A.D.V.S.
20TH DIVISION.

AV/35

Place	Date	Hour	Summary of Events and Information	Remarks and references to Appendices
Pan	1/9		Visit to M.V.S. & office Routine	
	2/9		Examined 25 + 2 cols. bef. under patch to Pans	
	3/9		Mallein mallein sent to 12 animals of R.A. Hqs	
	4/9		Mallein mallein sent to 21 animals of 60 squa ambne ammale ambulances at MARIEUX	
	5/9		Examined X & mes & ammals ambulances	
	6/9		Visit to M.V.S. & No 3 aug. bde	
	7/9		Sale of 2 animals at Pan	
	8/9		Visit 6 m Juyn. V. ade	
	9/9		Office Routine	
	10/9		Visit to 9 + No. 8 R. Ha.	
	11/9		Examined 39 + horses bef. embarkation at MARIEUX	
	12/9		Examined 47 cavalry horses " " " MARIEUX	
	13/9		Visit Aug. 9 & No. R. Aa.	

WAR DIARY
or
INTELLIGENCE SUMMARY.

Army Form C. 2118.

D.A.D.V.S.
20th DIVISION.

(Erase heading not required.)

Instructions regarding War Diaries and Intelligence Summaries are contained in F. S. Regs., Part II. and the Staff Manual respectively. Title pages will be prepared in manuscript.

Place	Date	Hour	Summary of Events and Information	Remarks and references to Appendices
Par.	14/10		Capt C. M. Semester R.A.V.C. (?) to dep't Mov'm'e admitted to mont'd to M? the D.A.C.	
	15/10		Visit to give hay, rations + m'o, the D.A.C.	
	16/10		Visits to m'o + offices r ormn	
	17/10		the arrival 146 x annex. mn't ambul'ce + remn.	
	18/10		Sunday (No.1) remove to Cocine Fruje.	

A. S. Blair
Coln R.A.V.O
aDaDVS. 20th Divn

www.ingramcontent.com/pod-product-compliance
Lightning Source LLC
Chambersburg PA
CBHW081423160426
43193CB00013B/2180